LIBRARY
KIRKWOOD COMMUNITY COLLEGE
6301 KIRKWOOD BLVD SW
CEDAR RAPIDS IA 52406

© Copyright 2005 Martin Laprise.
All rights reserved. No part of this publication may be reproduced, stored in a retrieval system, or transmitted, in any form or by any means, electronic, mechanical, photocopying, recording, or otherwise, without the written prior permission of the author.

Note for Librarians: A cataloguing record for this book is available from Library and Archives Canada at www.collectionscanada.ca/amicus/index-e.html
ISBN 1-4120-7068-6

Offices in Canada, USA, Ireland and UK
This book was published *on-demand* in cooperation with Trafford Publishing. On-demand publishing is a unique process and service of making a book available for retail sale to the public taking advantage of on-demand manufacturing and Internet marketing. On-demand publishing includes promotions, retail sales, manufacturing, order fulfilment, accounting and collecting royalties on behalf of the author.

Book sales for North America and international:
Trafford Publishing, 6E–2333 Government St.,
Victoria, BC v8T 4P4 CANADA
phone 250 383 6864 (toll-free 1 888 232 4444)
fax 250 383 6804; email to orders@trafford.com
Book sales in Europe:
Trafford Publishing (UK) Limited, 9 Park End Street, 2nd Floor
Oxford, UK OX1 1HH UNITED KINGDOM
phone 44 (0)1865 722 113 (local rate 0845 230 9601)
facsimile 44 (0)1865 722 868; info.uk@trafford.com
Order online at:
trafford.com/05-1979
10 9 8 7 6 5 4 3 2 1

Table of Contents

About the Author........................ 6
Acknowledgements.................... 7
Preface.. 8

Part one: The Ingredients
Introduction................................ 10
First of all 11
Lets start here 14
School is a must........................ 21
Qualities of a cook.................... 25
Qualities of a chef..................... 29
The 7 types of personalities..... 33

Part two: The Dough
Creativity.................................... 40
Work schedules......................... 43
Unionized kitchen...................... 45
Tarte au Sucre 50
Money... 51
Management.............................. 57
Trying out................................... 65
Beware, heads up, watch out ... 68
Can I speak to the chef ?.......... 77

3

Part three: The Bread
Job search.................................. 90
Ask your next employer 92
The choices.…............................ 97
- The French restaurant…..... 97
- The ethnic restaurant…...... 99
- The five diamond restaurants..................... 100
- The small bistro................ 102
- The breakfast and brunch restaurant 102
- The 24 hour restaurant 103
- The Tapas restaurant 104
- The employee's cafeteria … 104
- The school cafeteria …....... 106
- The hospital 107
- The corporate Chef........... 108
- The specialty restaurant 108
- The private Chef............... 110
- The personal Chef............ 110
- The fishing boat................ 111
- The cruise ship work 112
- The winery 114
- The truck stop................. 114
- The restaurant chain......... 115
- The bar and pub 115
- The private caterer …........ 116
- The movie caterer …......... 117
- The canteen truck 120
- The hotel banquet and restaurant 122

4

- The resort 124
- The spa.................. 126
- The banquet hall 127
- The private club/golf club ... 128
- The army kitchen 128
- The airline catering 129
- The summer camp 130
- The oil rig, and bush camp............................... 131
- The heli-ski 132
- The B&B........................... 132
- The sport stadium 133
- The mall food court restaurant 134
- The office building's snack bar................................ 134
- The gospel kitchen 135
- The cooking school 135

Part four: The Sandwich
Wrapping up..............................138
References............................... 141

The Author

Chef Martin Laprise has experience in culinary art and pastry art – a career that spans over 20 years, working in Quebec, Alberta, British Columbia and the Caribbean.

Over the years, Martin has worked in restaurants, cafeterias, banquet halls, movie catering, pastry shops, cruise ships, AAA 4 diamond fine dining rooms, and as a private chef cooking Greek food, Italian, Canadian, American, French, Asian and more... all this during breakfast, lunch or dinner.

One of the things in life that bothers Martin is when he sees talented cooks and chefs wasting away in a concept that is wrong for them just because they have not been guided on a career path that makes sense to them individually. "Every one has different personal skills, and those skills are crucial to anyone's success if they are used correctly, I love the idea of helping cooks and chefs" says Martin.

Martin has reached a point in his career where he wants to help as many people as possible find the real pluses and minuses of working in professional kitchens.

Acknowledgements

Thank you to Kristin, my wife, who provides me with great support, patience, love and spell check. To my daughter Chloae, who came into my life and changed me forever - this is for you!

Thanks to Marina Roggeveen for being so pushy and supportive years ago. Thanks to Sue Dagenais for her figure painting talents. Merci Yves Couture, Sylvie Beland, Micheline Gamache, Bertrand Laprise, et Bruno Manlhiot pour votre support depuis longtemps. Thanks to Barbara King, who helped me see my full potential. A special thanks goes to Lori Harrison for our conversation at the dentist's office, which led to this book.

To all the cooks, Chefs, dishwashers and waiters that I have worked with over the years, this book is made of our experiences together. I agree it was not always fun and games, but it is sure full of great memories.

Finally, thanks Therese, Marcel and Paul, wherever you are!

Preface

This book is the culmination of many years of Martin's efforts to share his passion with anyone willing to listen. It is truly a burning desire in him to pass along the secrets of his craft and to see the spark of new inspiration grow in the eyes of a new cook.

Food has always meant more to me than just necessary nourishment; it is a bridge that brings us all closer, at family gatherings or across cultures. Perhaps it is my appreciation for those experiences that led me to marry a Chef, and my reverence for his profession that makes Martin call me his muse. But the thing I love the most is that he exemplifies the Chef's version of that old Chinese proverb: "Give a man a fish and you feed him for a day. Teach a man to cook a fish and you feed him for a lifetime."

Kristin Peturson-Laprise

PART ONE
THE INGREDIENTS

Introduction

Dear reader,

Last night my daughter Chloae came to me and told me that she wanted to be a Chef when she was tall and old. I did not know what to say, as her Papa. Since she was born, I have wondered what profession she would choose for herself, but I never thought it would happen so soon, not now, not at 11 years old! I had a mixture of feelings - being extremely proud, and at the same time, extremely scared that I had given her the wrong impression about my career choice.

So, this book is for her, but it is also perfect for anybody who is thinking of a culinary career, or for the up-coming Chef needing a bit of guidance on choosing where to be a cook, or what kind of Chef to be.

Although my career choice of becoming a Chef has always served me right and rarely left me unemployed, this Papa has had a vision of something much more "bigger than life" for his only little girl.

At this point, I am not sure that I would want her, my only child, to start on this path before giving her a realistic picture of this amazing and yes, sometimes very challenging industry.

I love my job and it was the right choice for me, my only worry is that some kid would wants to be a chef for the wrong reasons.

Just like in most other books you will find a few spelling or syntax mistakes in my book. Please accept my apology in advance. I learn English on my own watching TV "Cheers and Night Court". You can make that your first lesson; nothing is perfect in life, not even the chef☺

First of all

I want to reassure you, Chloae, this book may seem like tough love at times, or even on the negative side. One thing that I have found out over the years is that people in general won't tell you the truth in fear of hurting your feelings. In my case, it is more important to me that you really see all the challenges that you may face everyday. Once you finish reading this book, you will have a better understanding of Papa's work. A culinary career can be a great choice, as long as you get in with your eyes open and have no false ideas. Over and over, I have seen young cooks start their culinary career thinking that they will be the next Julia Child or Emeril. While it is possible and sometimes does happen, it is not that common. As you will notice in a few pages, I often choose to show you very plainly the less fun part, or the inside track, of the culinary industry. Since you have probably heard and/or seen through the media so much more information about the glamorous things of being a Chef, many times in this book, I have chosen to tell you the things that they won't tell you in the movies or at school. But I am sharing all of this because I loved being a cook, and I love being a Chef even more. If this is your choice, go for it.

Let's start here

50 years ago, the Executive Chef in a hotel was a bigger than life persona, who was mostly seen as a master behind the stove. Usually a great leader with an attitude, the Chef would worry mostly about food and very little about the quality of relationship he/she had with the cooks. Basically, the Chef would rarely talk to you unless you screwed up. However, on the upside the hotels would usually provide a great environment for a free education. Profits were not the main goal; instead, getting customers to stay at the hotel was the main objective.

Well, times change! Today's Chef needs to be able to lead the cooks in a very different way than before. The Chef has to be an expert in the area of Human Resources, respect labour laws, reduce staff turnover to keep training costs down, and keep the labour cost on track. Today's Chef also needs to able to control food cost to very specific target, read financial spreadsheets, and obviously make profits. As in any work place in this world, efficiency has become the main word in the kitchen. Knowing all that, you can imagine the skills you will need to get an Executive Chef job in 10 or 20 years from now!

Before you get to be a Chef, you will need to be a good cook for a few years. Everyday of your life you will be faced with decisions, and a big part of those will be made based on your work. Directly or indirectly, your family is also going to dictate some of your choices, money and schedule being the big ones. For example, you cannot do a 9-5 schedule at a fine dining French restaurant, even if you own it… Those restaurants open at night, therefore you will work at night and you will rarely be at the table for dinner with your own family. On the other hand, if you work in a breakfast-only concept, it will allow you to be home and help with your children's school homework. The only thing is, you won't be cooking any masterpieces with eggs.

Hopefully money is not why you want to be a Chef, but of course keep in mind that your landlord will be coming each month for his share of the pot, so it has its importance. Most professional Chefs do it for the rewards coming from the customers, or to create works of art, or for the challenges that working in the kitchen brings everyday. Others do it because working in a team environment can really give you a sense of belonging to something bigger than just you. The adrenaline rush before the service is comparable to sky diving. It's a great profession and one thing is for sure, not everyone needs a lawyer, but people eat everyday and will continue to do so for many more years to come. So while you make your choice, keep in mind that some careers will have better money than others. You may not be able to buy your husband a new car for Christmas, but cooking should allow you to live a comfortable life.

Your location can be challenging sometimes! Working in a resort town is great, but it is not always easy to buy pieces of over priced property or even raise a family there, if that is your choice. Working in the city is great too, but harder to pass through interviews, as many people living in the city center want those same jobs.

A huge advantage with a culinary career can be that your cooking skills may be common in your country, but not so much in others. Chefs are in big demand all over the world, and this may create some great opportunities to travel to places like Africa, Ireland, Bermuda or Afghanistan.

Benefits will be better at certain jobs, whether you like the job or not! But you may need to stay working for a certain concept until you finish with your children's dental work. These are choices that I faced everyday.

Staying physically fit and mentally healthy is very important in our industry.

A word of advice; find yourself an exercise routine that fits with your life style, and a stress relieving hobby.

Learning by example is the best way, so seek a mentor that can teach you the true values that all great Chefs need to be successful.

Compared to other careers, your culinary career will never run out - there will never be a machine that can replace a great Chef! Thirty years from now, Chefs will still cook with pots and pans and great food will still be in big demand. Fortunately for us, the food industry jobs are growing by almost 15% every year all over the world. How's that for job security!

I like small restaurants, as you can see every workstation from your own work area. This makes things easier to learn, as you can just look up to know what are the other cooks are doing. In the large kitchen you have more positions to aim for once you are ready for a promotion, but also more cooks to compete against. In smaller establishments, you may very often need to leave in order to learn more.

Kitchens can drive you crazy some days. Always keep emotion out of it while making decisions. You can scream once you get in your car or cry once you get home. Whatever you do, don't keep it inside, always deal with your feelings in a timely fashion.

Never forget, the one big advantage to becoming a Chef is simple; you will never have to go hungry again.

A word of advice: never quit a job before you have another one lined up… Rent is always due at the end of the month, even if you're not working.

No matter which jobs you choose, which locations, or which concepts, you will always learn something. Even if you only learn that you don't like doing this or that, you are learning. One problem that can happen is if you stay doing something you don't like too long and become unhappy doing it. Learn to make yourself happy by finding the job for you. Chefs move around, it's a fact. If you move too much, you are seen as not stable - not enough, and you are seen as inexperienced! Find a happy middle that fits for you.

Anywhere you work and whatever profession you choose, you will always find good things and bad things about your job. Focus on the good stuff, make the best out of what you have and don't stay working at a job you don't like more than you have to! I have a good example of that for you...

While I worked at this hotel in a Banff resort, I used to feel pretty shitty during the Christmas season. You were in Vancouver and I was a 12-hour drive away from you. So, I did what I had to do to keep my sanity and my Christmas spirit - I volunteered in the "Annual Christmas Parade". Basically, from December 15 or so, until 25 December at 7pm sharp when we actually got to send Santa away on his journey around the world. The idea was to walk around the halls of the hotel dressed up in a special suit and meet all the kids that were staying with us. We had Santa Claus and Mrs. Claus, a Toy Soldier, A Fairy, a Gingerbread Man, two Elves, Rudolph the Red-nosed Reindeer (which was Kristin) and I was dressed up in a big Frosty the Snowman suit made with thick white, furry carpet-like kind of material. It was so freakin' hot that the sweat from top of my head would roll into my eyes. The problem was that I couldn't remove my head to wipe my eyes, because Frosty was so popular that I almost always had a kid hanging on to Frosty's leg! Have you ever heard the saying, "One hour a day, keeps the Christmas blues away"? I still missed your presence, but it made my work so much more fun during these tough times. During the rest of the year, Kristin and I got to teach ballroom dancing lessons to the staff of the hotel, and that was fun too! Overall, our time at the resort was full of great unique experiences, mostly because of our outside activities that made work go by so quickly.

   Keep reading, darling, and let me know if you have any questions. I'll be in the kitchen, cooking breakfast.

School is a must

If you are wondering if school is important in becoming a good Chef, the answer is yes... I would recommend you to take a two-year program minimum, and three years is even better. Culinary schools are like any other trade school, some you don't know and in Canada are free, and some others cost and have a reputation that will most definitely help you down the road to employment. This trade is like any other artistic trade: it's what you do with it that counts. Once you finish school, you still have to learn how to work in a kitchen, but in a more practical way instead of on paper. This is where it gets interesting.

A word of advice: once you enter the work force, don't talk about what school you came from or how good you were in school, your co-workers don't really care and they will ask you if they want to know!

The best schools to my knowledge will be the ones that offer apprenticeship programs where they mix school with actual work in the industry. My favorite programs alternate 2 months at school, then 2 months at work for two or three years.

A word of advice: the more hours you spend at school learning about your trade the better prepared you will be when you enter the work force.

Just so you can compare, an engineer in computer robotics that just finished university will have put in around 8000 to 10,000 hours to learn their trade. They will usually make great money right out of school. If you spend two or three years (4000 to 6000 hours) in a culinary school, even if you come out number one of your class, you can expect just OK money to start. So, while you are at school, it is very important that you really get involved and spend all your time thinking about your trade and learn as much as you can. That way, you are giving yourself the best chances. It's much easier to ask an employer for more money if you are at the top your trade, and much harder for an employer to justify the money if you are just average.

Honey, don't be average, be all that you can be.

A word of advice: It's OK to stay an extra half hour after work just to learn a new technique - it will only make you a better Chef. All Chefs all over the world have given away unpaid time to learn more; it's the nature of the business.

Often, the school will have special events that need volunteers – if so, do it. You will learn so much more working those events instead of sitting on your couch after school. Many schools will have a small restaurant inside the school to allow the students to learn hands-on what it is really like to work in a restaurant. Those school restaurants will give you valuable experience right before you go out in the real world.

A word of advice: Learn your culinary terms, and don't be shy to learn many classic recipes, as they will be useful. It's always nice to know the answer when the Chef asks a question, as it puts you on the Chef's right side as opposed to the other option.

If you have the choice to learn about business, accounting, computers, and financial report reading during your school time, take it. The more you are prepared for a big job, the faster you will get there and the better you will do!

A word of advice: Learn to use your knives at school ASAP - it's the number one thing to know! Once you have good control of your knives, learn every cooking technique there is to know, and practice every time you can so you really feel comfortable when the time comes to show off your skills to your new Chef.

You will have to keep reading food magazines to stay up to date with trends, flavors and presentation styles. This career choice is very exciting if you know your trade, and it's very frustrating if you don't have the skills.

Qualities of a Cook

Before you become a Chef, you will be a cook until you can take charge of the whole kitchen. The cook is the person who works for the Chef.

All successful cooks have many qualities or commonalities, but the two things that come out the most are their dedication to improve their culinary skills and the tenacity to stay the course even in highly stressful situations.

People skills are one very important asset in your toolbox as a cook. You will have to sell yourself to employers, customers and coworkers for the rest of your career. A person that is social, open minded, giving and out going is often a good candidate for a culinary career. It is absolutely crucial to be able to say you screwed up when you do, because you will screw up, trust me.

Knife skills are extremely important because you won't be able to go very fast unless you know how to use your knives. When I left school and for the next few years, every time I would start a new job, I would always slash one of my fingers on my first day and have to look for a Band-Aid.

A word of advice: don't take years to start carrying a Band-Aid in your toolbox. That way, you don't have to go ask the Chef once you cut your fingers.

Speed of execution is going to be your second best quality. Just get things done and move on to the next thing - employers will love that attitude.

A word of advice: If you ever end up with a huge mise-en-place list, a cranky Chef, and not so much time, the best place to gain time is on the kitchen floor, not on your cutting board. What I mean by that is, once you are already cutting as fast as you can, it's pretty hard to go even faster without chopping one of your fingers off. So between jobs, you can walk faster to get the food from the fridge for example, and/or always carry food back once you go pick something up. Don't work harder, work smarter!

A sense of humor will come in handy for the cook when the Chef starts laughing at you because you forgot the basic ingredients of a classic Mornay sauce. At the beginning of your career, you will be laughed at a lot, so grow a thick skin and learn to laugh at yourself. Everyone makes mistakes – just learn from them.

Initiative is a great quality to have in the kitchen. If you can foresee problems, you will always be ahead of your competition. Don't be shy to make a decision; employers should support you, as long as you don't burn the building down. Making decisions is something that you get good at once you practice, so be the decision maker every time you can.

Flexibility, and I don't mean to be able to touch your toes! The ability to adapt to your team's needs at any specific time is priceless. From the grill to the pastry station, or from the saucier to the dishwasher, be the one to save the day, and you should have a prosperous career.

Listening and concentration skills will be very important. If you concentrate on your work, and listen to what is happening around you, you will really be able to help your team score big. For example, I use to work at this small restaurant, and I knew that the Chef de Partie in charge was my ticket to a promotion. So, I would make sure that during service time he never had to wait for my stuff. I was on vegetables, and I was always ready a split second before he needed me. I got my promotion and eventually got his job.

A word of advice: keep your private life outside of work. It should help your concentration and performance. It's pretty simple, while at work you talk about work, and while at the pub you talk about whatever you want!

Punctuality is important, because the customers will not wait for you to show up. Your job's future will be very much dependant on you showing up on time.

Being a quick learner is a must. Without it you cannot advance fast enough to keep ahead of your coworkers' progress. Don't be shy to say you don't know something, and make sure to tell everyone you want to learn it right now!

Qualities of a Chef

The Chef gets to wear the tall hat and give directions to the cooks. Ultimately, though, the buck stops at the Chef!

Leadership qualities are going to be necessary to advance your career. It is an extremely important quality to be able to lead, even in a tough situation. Once you are the girl in charge at the front of the pack, every eye will be looking at you, so you will have to be composed, or at the very least look calm.

Diplomacy is a key factor in any Chef's toolbox. The art of firing someone politely is priceless. It's like being able to find a way to tell a customer that the reason his main course did not taste like lobster is because it was crabmeat, not lobster!

I've got to tell this, it's a great example. It's the winter of 1987 in Montreal, the evening was just about over, we have just fed the last table, and so like every night, I send one of my cooks home.

She leaves and comes back inside a few minutes later to tell us that one of the cars in our parking lot is running, but no one was inside. I thought that she was playing a joke on me because I made her do the Orange Tart on the menu where you need to zest 30 oranges and make a confit out of it. No, she was right, there was an empty car running outside. My partner and I play the rock-paper-scissors game and I lost, so a few minutes later in the half empty dining room... "Excuse me sir, your Jaguar is still running outside". His answer is, "Yes I know! I don't like to get in a cold car, so I left it running! And suddenly the dining room looked much more full to me - every table around heard him talking and I felt very stupid. It was one of those Chef days where diplomacy was useful, but I still looked stupid.

People skills are also a must for any Chef. Everyday you will be put in situations where your ability to use your social skills will be tested. Keeping an open mind and having the right attitude is going to get you out of trouble throughout your whole career. For example, the ability to listen to an employee's serious family issues is extremely important, even if it does not interest you at all. This is how you will gain the trusts and respect of your team members. Reading your team skills and knowing how to talk to people so they get the job done is a must in a Chef position.

A sense of humor for the Chef is also a must, especially when your cooks forget the basic ingredients of a classic Mornay sauce. If you lose it instead of laughing at them, it won't make your cooks learn the ingredients faster. Laughing is the second best stress relief on the planet.

Work Experience should be acquired before taking on too many responsibilities. Even if responsibility is thrown at you, I strongly suggest that you work at 3-5 different stations in 3-5 different establishments before taking on to much responsibility. Think of it like a good wine that needs to sit for while before achieving peek stage... as you get more experience, you are becoming a more complete Chef.

Creativity is the part that makes you want to be a Chef, so just use it! Read and stay in touch with the trends, find your groove and perfect it during your first 10 years in the kitchen. Go out and see what others are doing - it will open your eyes to the world and make you a better Chef. Shop at open markets every time you can, it's very inspiring...

Techniques will get you out of a jam more than once. Learn your trade, be all that you can be and join the front of the pack. There is nothing worse than a Chef who only knows one way of doing something.

Business sense is a funny one, because you can function without it as a cook, but as a Chef you need it to see financial trouble before it happens. If you ever have your own business, make sure that you know about every dollar spent.

A word of advice: The garbage will be your worst enemy, so make sure you don't over feed your worst enemy. Wastage greatly affects direct profit. Keep an eye on your cooks that throw away $3 of food on every shift, as it adds up to $1000 of dollars at the end of the year. Learn about the business world through examples, courses and books; trust me it will pay off at the end, in dollars.

The 7 major types of personalities

You will notice that in many cases you need to have multiple types of personalities to make a great cook or Chef, and you also need many types within your team. Like most things in life, a little bit of everything is often better than too much of one thing. The most successful cooks and Chefs around the world have developed into well adjusted human beings before they become cooks and/or Chefs. Let's face it, once you reach 25 to 30 years old, the bulk of your personality is fully developed and it becomes very hard to modify it. The core of your work ethic, sense of humour, temperament, mind-set, and your general approach to life is pretty much set. It's not impossible to change, but much harder. Once you know in which areas you can improve, start working on it, and you can only become a better person for it!

The Cooks:

The Know-it-All is the one that always has a better way to do things and he/she has to tell you about it. Annoying as hell, and often full of shit, but an OK choice compared to many others. Better to have a know-it-all than one that knows nothing...

The Shy One is often a cook that stays in one place for many years, and if you have too many of those types in your kitchen, it may slow down your growth. A cook that stays put too long often lacks creativity or drive, but a cook that knows when to shut up is a good thing too.

The Wanna-be thinks that he/she should be promoted from Day One. Watch out, anything goes -they often will try to make you look bad if you take too much of their spotlight. This type should not be promoted too fast, as it will only feed the monster inside - that big ego.

The Cook-to-Go to is your most even-tempered cook. This one is serious enough to take charge when needed, to make sure that the work gets done on time. A great team player, someone funny enough to keep your team uplifted all day. He/she will talk and think about work while at work. He/she will produce high quality food at a great speed.

Generally, this type is a cook that physically moves faster than the average person in the kitchen. If you are the Chef, delegate to this cook. No need to repeat your requests 5 times, as they will get done the first time. Fill up your kitchen with this type and you are home free as a Chef.

The Socially Unstable cook creates chaos in the kitchen. Not so good with customer service, this one is a time bomb waiting to explode. Even if this type of cook brings great technical skills to your team, you are playing with fire. Counseling is the best option, but hopefully not from the Chef. A cook with a short fuse is not very good to have around knives.

The Lifer is an average skilled cook that doesn't want to move up, but will give you a steady 65-75% effort until retirement. Without much initiative or drive, it's OK to have one or two of those, but if the kitchen is full of them, you will have a bunch of depressed cooks feeding off each other.

The Party Animal needs to grow up. This is a cook that starts the day by telling you the events from the night before and the prep-work will just have to wait. Often, and without noticing, the rest of the team may carry the workload for this cook just for the sheer entertainment. The kitchen is often like a summer camp for this one.

The Chefs:

The Artist only thinks about the food: people are just there to make the food look better. Rarely in the office doing paper work, the Artist is often not very organized, but creates great masterpieces. Not much for people skills, but combined with an Administrator and/or the Easy Going type of Chef, it can be a great combination.

The Screamer and/or Aggressive type needs a dose of craziness on a daily basis. It is strongly suspected that he/she may have fallen on their head sometime during their childhood. Overall, when people skills were distributed, the Screamer and Aggressive Chef did not get their fair share. If you find one of these Chefs, and they are already middle-aged or older, don't expect changes... this is it! Overall, this kind of Chef does not like people. Don't take it personally. I don't care how great these people are at cooking, they suck!

The Chef Owner will have some money invested in the restaurant, so he/she will be serious when it comes down to work, but also able to keep it fun, because he/she is usually very happy to work for herself/himself. Often a multi-tasker and some times a bit stressed out, he/she will run a tight ship. Food cost will be on track, menus kept up to date, they will teach you new techniques every other day, and in general they do like to work with people. This Chef is more levelheaded than any other type, and most often a great person from whom to learn your trade. Overall, this Chef is a good one to take as a mentor.

The Administrator is not often seen outside of his/her normal habitat, "the office". He/she lives in the office, eats in the office and usually only comes out to have a pee or go home. Yes, today more than ever, kitchens need to be productive and profitable, and yes, often that work starts in the office. So, usually the budget will be tightly run, but that Chef will not know where the carrots are kept in the kitchen. This is a great Chef if combined with a Teacher or an Easy Going type.

The Dumb Founded type is not usually a great one for delegating or managing people. This is a Chef that will be surprised when shit happens, even though he/she knew it could happen. They often want change, but can't tell you where to start. Not so good to be around if you have a short temper yourself, as they will frustrate you, a lot. The good thing is that they offer great entertainment for the experienced cooks.

The Easy Going type is a great boss for the cooks, but not always the best Chef or administrator. Don't get attached to this type, as they move a lot. Often not very on the ball when it comes to the numbers and/or food quality, they either get fired or they quit first. However, the Easy Going type is great when combined with an Artist and/or Administrator.

The Teacher will be the best choice if you like to learn new stuff. The Teacher will make your day go fast, and will often be someone who likes people, not a bad quality to have in the kitchen. Most of the time you can find this one in the kitchen with a cook watching closely. Again, this type combined with an Administrator creates a powerful Chef.

PART TWO
THE DOUGH

Creativity or Not

I do believe that cooking jobs in most professional kitchens can be divided in two categories: the jobs where you can create a lot and the ones where you cannot create at all.

Creative jobs are great, but can add stress to your day. Whether you have to make a different special every day, or whether you need to make new menus every 3 months, being creative demands talents, time and it does add stress. The cool part is that you get to try new stuff and use the other side of your brain once in while.

I have always been attracted to the creative side of things, but a few times in my career, to stay employed, I had to be the non-creative, shut-up and do-your-job person.

Many times, when you put too many creative people together in a small space, there will be sparks. As a cook, you will need to develop a thick skin for these types of positions, and as a Chef you should try to hire a mixture of talents. Your coworkers and/or boss will not always agree with your creativity, and they will let you know how much they don't like it. Deal with it and move on! Customers can be brutally honest some times, and this can be very hard if you work in an open concept kitchen where you talk to customers all day. Just remember, not everyone likes peanut butter and pickle sandwiches!

Non-creative jobs will not be as stressful, but can be very repetitive on a daily basis. Often, menus have been established years ago, and/or new items will be made by the corporate Chef in a test kitchen somewhere else.

Once you start your culinary career, most employers will appreciate your opinion, but most of the time they will not implement your ideas, just because you are to fresh out of school. Keep speaking up, and one day they will listen.

Non-creative environments can make some staff bitter, and as a result, they become not-so-friendly coworkers to be around. In many cases, the non-creative positions are in a unionized kitchen but not always... places like hospitals, corporate chain restaurants, airline caterers, many hotels etc...

A word of advice: Try both environments and see which one is the best fit for you. Some people like the routine work, and others like to do something different every other day.

Work Schedules

When it comes down to schedules, you will have many choices. Whether you want full time, part-time or occasional work, your schedule may well be different at every job you do! Some kitchens operate one, two or three meals a day, while others are 24/7 operations, 365 days a year.

There is some contract work that asks you to do a specific task like creating a menu and that's it. There is other contract work where you work everyday for a few weeks or a few months, and then you get time off until your next contract. Sometimes you do day shift one week then night shift the next week, other times you do only breakfast and you get to be home every night for dinner. Banquet and catering work is often on-call type work, and French restaurants are mostly night work. The smaller the kitchen is, the less flexible the schedule will be. The bigger the kitchen is, the more policies there are about changing your schedule. I strongly suggest that you choose your work according to the schedule attached to that position. Your personal life is extremely important, and it should dictate your work life schedule - make sure that it's not the other way around.

Unionized kitchen or Not

This will be one of the major choices you will need to make as a cook. It is necessary in order to find the perfect match for you.

How do you decide the type of kitchen for you? Well, I will attempt to give you some impartial examples from both sides, although I personally had to make that choice a long time ago.

The Unionized kitchen
This concept is often in big kitchens and/or big companies. Sometimes it is very hard to find a unionized job due to the demand compare to the offer. Many people choose the union as the way to go! Many reasons come to mind... security of employment is the biggest one usually, as it is much harder to be fired, even when you do mediocre work. Money can also be seen as an advantage, as the cook's wages usually start a bit higher, and as whole, money

is good. The biggest draw for most unionized workers are employee benefits like medical and dental coverage, life insurance, sick days, stock options and increasing vacation time just to name a few!

In general in a unionized kitchen, before you start, you will have completed many interviews, written many paper forms and met a union leader that explained to you the in's and out's of your rights as a union member.

Usually, you would also complete a few hours of training for your new position, and get the grand tour of your new workspace. You will have to complete a probation period to guarantee your employment, usually around 3 months. You should show off your stuff in the first couple weeks, as the employer may try to fire you before your probation is over if you don't perform well enough. After that, it will be fairly hard for your employer to fire you; the union will always fight for your rights instead of you doing it. If you run into a problems with your employer during your shift, it is required that a union leader be present to help you resolve any issues.

Once you start your first official shift, everything will be explained very clearly to you … about cigarette breaks, lunch breaks, afternoon breaks and any other rights that you have and should take advantage of, on a regular basis. You will need to learn to cook the way the establishment requires obviously, but that is very common in any kind of kitchen.

Unionized kitchens will create certain issues that you may not want to deal with on a regular basis. Schedules are always a big deal, your co-workers will study and sometimes memorize your schedule before they look at their own, just to make sure that you did not get a shift that should have been offered to them first. It sounds simple, but after a while, trust me, it can get on your nerves. Now, in general, the actual work mentality is different! When your shift is done, you will have to stop working and go home, as the next worker will finish what you have started... It does not matter what it is, you will be asked to leave immediately. Picture this: Leonardo DaVinci is painting his famous masterpiece, and someone taps him on the shoulder and says, "Go home, your shift is over, I will finish your Mona Lisa for you!" This should tell you why often these jobs are not creative based jobs.

If you were thinking that you could just finish your vegetable platter and then you would go home, think again.

Someone will place a grievance complain about you because you are taking the work of someone else, resulting in problems for you. Although your employment is relatively secure, you still want to try to stay away from negative paper work.

It is true that a union kitchen tends to be a more controlled, sterile environment. For example, if you are cooking in a restaurant that is part of a chain, and you want to make sure that everyone in the company receives equal opportunity, union will do that for you!

The non-unionized kitchen
Usually small kitchens would be non-union, but not always.

In this case, you can still have other kinds of issues that can be annoying. The hiring process is often much simpler, although it is becoming more thorough. The interview should be quick and easy, and you may even be asked to start right away or the next morning, sometimes without training.

You will also have to complete a probation period to guarantee your employment, usually, also around 3 months. You should show off your speed and talents in the first few weeks, because your rights are pretty much non-existent until your probation is over. The good thing is a non-unionized kitchen will usually, but not always be slower to fire your ass and a touch more patient with your lack of skills or speed, as many times people are not lining up to get your job. After your probation, your employment may be ended fairly easily, but you will have to defend your own self, as no union leader will be there to fight for you. Usually, you will have to ask for a raise, as it won't come automatically as it often does in a unionized establishment. The work environment can be a bit more relaxed, and you will be allowed to finish your vegetable platter without anyone writing you a grievance! Your schedule is not going to be the big focus of your co-workers. You may have a hard time getting sick days off from your employer, and vacation is also often frowned upon. Although a small restaurateur may not want you to go on vacation, it is the law! The problem with small businesses is if you are part of a team of 4 cooks, once one cook is gone, 25% of the labor force is gone... That could mean a big deal on a Saturday night. The work can be great, if you have a good team and co-workers willing to show you stuff... In a small, non-unionized restaurant for example, you can stay after your shift on your own time to learn something new, but not in a unionized kitchen.

This is Papa's famous dessert, so you get at least one recipe out of this book. I grew up on this stuff and let me tell you, it's sweet but it's good…

Quebec's Tarte au Sucre (Sugar Pie)

This recipe makes two 9" Pies

Ingredient:

2 cups of Brown Sugar

¼ cup Flour

1 Egg

1 can Carnation Milk 2%

¼ lb unsalted Butter

A touch of Vanilla

Method:

Pre-cook your 9" piecrust for 6-8 minutes at 350F

Melt the butter and set aside.

Beat at medium speed the brown sugar, milk and egg.

In a bowl, mix together butter and flour.

Mix together both mixtures and poor into your pre-cooked pie crusts and cook at the bottom of your oven at 350F until they are dry on top and look nice and golden.

Eat it with vanilla ice cream, breakfast, lunch or dinner!

Money

I hope that money is not why you want to become a Chef, and if so, someone has fed you the wrong information. To really sum it up, the best example I can give you is this:

If you take a lawyer, a computer analysts or a carpenter, after 20 years of doing a great job working for others, you can expect those three professionals to be making great money. They will usually own a house on top of the hill, including a pool with a view and a garage for both cars. Their kids will be in private school and on the weekends they will drive to the country house with six of their closest friends.

After 20 years of being a cook and then a Chef in all kinds of kitchens doing an amazing job, you can expect to be making OK to great money if you are very lucky. You may own a house, but it will most likely be at the bottom of the hill or you may not even see the hill at all from where you live. Your view is going to be of your neighbor's pink plastic flamingoes on the lawn and their pit bull. Your car will probably be on the street surrounded by snow with everyone else, and when you go to the countryside, you will be camping. Your kids are definitely not going to private school, but once they come out of school detention, they should be fine. No, really, jokes aside, in our trade, 65-70% of salaries are in the low to medium range at best. Think about it, an executive chef can make great money, but there is only per restaurants, all the other salaries in the kitchen are below!

So you ask yourself why become a Chef? Well, it's simple - so the lawyers, computer geeks and carpenters have a place to go eat!

A word of advice: In general, being a Chef and owning your own restaurant is not a get-rich quick kind of career move. The chances of you actually making serious money before you want to commit suicide are very slim. It's a great experience to live through, but don't get into it for the money.

Obviously, you should not expect to make great money coming out of school; you will have to work your way up the ranks before you can afford to buy a

Ferrari!

In general, the big places will pay you more than the small places.

<u>A word of advice:</u> No need to talk about money on your first interview. Find out if this place is for you first, and does it match your talents and will it make you grow into a better Chef. If you do decide to take the job, then ask about money, and don't sell yourself cheap.

Throughout the entire book, I will use the following terms to describe the money potential of that particular job. Keep in mind that these numbers are relative, because in some cases, you may be able to bypass the norm and get more money based on experience, luck and/or the desperation of the employer. I have seen cooks on the East coast making 15-20% less than on the West coast for the same type jobs. Being in a small town can also bring the salary down, as it is more of a captive audience, and many people want your job. The opposite can also happen, if you are the only chef available in town, it would pay off

Depending on the company, some will pay you weekly, bi-weekly, bi-monthly, once a month, or on a contract basis. I always disliked the once-a-month format, as I prefer to have my money sitting in my account instead of the wealthy employer's account.

<u>A word of advice:</u> It is up to you to make sure that no mistakes are made on your pay cheques. Even accountants make mistakes. Depending on where you work, you may have to use an electronic punching clock, or a computerized magnetic card, or some other device not invented yet. Trust me when I say this: <u>Always</u> keep track in writing and on a daily basis of the hours you work. These tricks will save you many arguments with the payroll person. One forgotten hour a week at $10 an hour for a year will add up to $520 at the end of the year.

Listed below is the money breakdown for my relative scale. Keep in mind that these dollar figures are in US dollars, and figures can vary depending on the different countries or cities where you live, or where you are planning to go work.

Amazing money for a Chef; $70,000 or more a year
  Great money is $40,000 to $70,000
  Good money is $28,000 to $40,000
  OK money is $20,000 to $28,000
  Not so good money would be below $20,000. This is what you should expect when you are starting your career.

The expatriate money package can be great if you like traveling around the world. You will often be well paid per hour or salary and have free housing included. One example that comes to mind was this company looking for a sous-Chef with 10 years experience. You would work in Africa, you would get paid in US dollars, but the money was being deposited into a bank account in England (how's that for complex?) The tax laws in England may be somewhat different than where you live, and may offer some financial advantages - or not - when you re-enter your own country with your money. The tax laws can change every year in every country, so do some research before accepting any deal that sounds too good to be true.

A word of advice: It is not so smart to accept to be paid a wage in cash "under the table". First, if you get caught, it could mean serious trouble and second, if you ever want to borrow money for a house for example, the cash money you get won't be shown anywhere. So the bank may tell you that you don't make enough money to get your loan, even if you know you can pay for it.

You can expect to be making very good money after 7 to 12 years, obviously, depending on decisions you will make earlier in your career.

<u>A word of advice:</u> Start saving 5% to 10% from each pay cheque, starting at day one. Once the money is in your account, retirement money grows while you sleep, but don't be sleeping on the switch. Save from day one and you too can afford a condo in the Bahamas.

Some benefits can make up for less money on your pay cheque. Things like discounts in hotels around the world, fitness card memberships, stock options, traveling expenses to get to work, or a company car... just to name a few.

<u>A word of advice:</u> As a cook, the best thing you can do with some of your money would be to invest some of it ASAP. The bulk of the culinary positions around the world will only make OK to good money. Knowing these facts, it is best to invest into assets that gain value instead of things like cars or rental apartments that lose value every year. Once you find an employer that fits your long term needs, buying a house or condo nearby is one of the best moves you will ever make as a cook or Chef. Seek professional financial help.

Management or not

Once you reach a certain culinary level and you feel ready for a different kind of challenge, you may want to become part of management - "The Chef". Believe me, it's always fun to tell people what to do!

You will have to develop your own management style, so pay attention during the beginning of your career and learn how to talk to people. You could be a great person, but your cooks won't necessarily work for you. On the other hand if your cooks hate you, you have another bunch of problems. So, find your own style just between soft and tough, or fair and square! Offer support and understanding to your team and they will work for you. Treat people with respect and they will work for you. And remember it's OK to be tough when needed; after all, it is your neck on the line.

Depending on where you work, management positions in the kitchen are usually less hands-on, and they start including office work like making menus, hiring, firing, scheduling, ordering and inventory and more...

As a rule of thumb, the more you go up in kitchen hierarchy, the less often you peel carrots. For example, most Executive Chefs in big kitchens rarely cook; those positions become more administrative work, and usually more important through the eyes of higher management, the corporation and/or owners. The pressure to control each dollar usually takes precedence over creativeness. The fun of making a menu is replaced by the fun of hitting labour cost targets and receiving a bonus for it.

A word of advice: Your net pay, or take-home money, is going to be better in a management position. Don't ever calculate what it adds up to per hour worked, though, as it is enough to make you want to quit!

You will not be paid hourly any more; instead, most of those positions will pay you on a fixed salary per year. You will be expected to do enough hours to assure a smooth operating kitchen. You will be asked to keep a flexible schedule, working weekends, busy nights, holidays and all special events - in a nutshell, nearly every day.

If you have the right personality, supervising a kitchen can be challenging, fun and very rewarding. It's great to see your team reach a higher level of skills because of your leadership. If you don't have the right personality, managing a kitchen can be your worst nightmare, and it can really make you fed up with cooking, to a point where you may even want to become a computer geek. As for women in the kitchen, unfortunately even today, the kitchen is still mostly a man's world. There will be extra challenges for you to get respected. "I have no doubt that my little girl can do it."

Leading is not for everyone, and that's just fine! A word of advice: only take a supervising position when you feel ready for it deep down in your gut, and you know that your executive Chef will be supportive and a great mentor. Ultimately, it is in your Chef's best interest to set you up for success, as you will represent his will in the kitchen.

Your best skill will be to treat people the way you want to be treated. Try to remember where you came from, and remember when you were a non-management employee. Do not be scared to say you don't know something. It's normal, just stay calm and be a leader. Delegate and empower your cooks to make decisions; they will feel important and most of the time, they will make you look good. Create relationships with your team based on trust and respect. Teach them to have fun at work; a la carte menus can get repetitive. Challenge them to create new stuff every time you can, as it will pay off at the end. Interact with your team outside of work hours, but keep it professional, they will love it! Ultimately, the performance of the team is a direct reflection on the leader's ability to keep them focused, motivated and interested.

One great piece of management advice I can give you is when you need to talk to one of your cooks about a performance issue, use the following steps:

1- Find a quiet place so you don't get disturbed.

2- Be positive in your opening, talk about the cook's strong points and don't say "but" at end, as it usually announces bad news. Just use something like this: "While we value your skills, we have found that you could improve in this or that…" The use of the word "WE" instead of I makes it less personal.

3- Give the cook a chance to respond to your comments, because everyone likes to be heard. Listen and make sure that you show interest in what the cook has to say - you will sometimes learn valuable information about your kitchen. Stay on course and make sure that the improvements needed are presented simply and are easy to understand.

4- After you have outlined where the improvement needs to be made, just reiterate the cook's strong points and the fact that only a small effort needs to be made to reach that level. No one wants to leave this kind of meeting having a feeling like the necessary improvement cannot be attained. Break it down into small goals!

5- Make sure that you are available to coach and provide extra support to that cook. Always set a follow up meeting for another sit down talk, to show the cook that you are serious about this process.

6- Always keep records of those sit-down talks, as it can be of use to map out their progress and/or show the cook how much more there is still to be done. These records can also be of use to demonstrate to the cook who won't try hard enough that this is the reason why termination is the only solution left!

As a leader in the kitchen, you will be respected if you work at it. Once you have a cook that is not working well with the rest of the team, it is up to you to fix it! If you do nothing, the rest of the team will lose respect for you, and the entire team's work will suffer. On the other hand, if you take care of the bad apple professionally, then your team will look up to you. You don't have to fire the cook, just kick the crap out of them. Jokes aside, it is your job to take care of your team!

The one thing that will define your job when you become management is simply the power to hire and fire someone. At some point, you will have to hire cooks. Just remember, they will work for you. If you don't think that this person is made to work with you and your team, just don't hire that person. Use your own judgment, and 95% of the time you will be right. Most great Chefs hire cooks on personality traits, skills, and experience, in that order. You can teach someone how to make a sauce, but it is much harder to teach someone how to be a well-adjusted human being. Everywhere I had to hire someone, I came up with one question that was way out there just to see his or her reaction. Example; what do you think of ACDC? Or If I called your last Chef right now, what would he/she say about you? Or, did you like the movie "Forest Gump"? These questions always get them talking, just so you can see their personality and body language.

Once you enter the world of management, you will have to sit down and have meetings on a regular basis with people of other nationalities and backgrounds. Don't be an ass by opening your mouth a bit too quickly, just listen and learn at the beginning. Once you feel comfortable you can start voicing your opinions, but keep in mind that not everyone will like to hear what you have to say. Keep emotion out of it, and say we instead of I, so that your comments come out as less confrontational.

A word of advice: Once you are the Chef, it is your responsibility to make sure that your cooks interact efficiently with all serving staff. You need to teach honesty and respect towards the front of the house. A cook without servers is just like an omelet without eggs - they need each other.

Your best pals at work may stop liking you once you have to sit down with them regarding their constant lateness. It is very important for you to keep in mind that when you take on a management position, it will be perceived by your coworkers as jumping over to the other side of the fence.

A word of advice: Once you start in a new place and before making strong relationships at work, keep in mind that you may become their boss someday. It is much easier as a manager if you had kept some distance, but that is one reason why management is not for everyone. I strongly advise you to prepare yourself by reading good management books before making that jump. If you want to get anywhere as a Chef, you will have to become the leader one day. You rarely hear about the cooks who were behind the scene.

Trying out

People will spend hours trying out shoes before finally buying a pair. When it comes down to your career, you should spend the same amount of energy as when you shop for shoes!

A word of advice: Get yourself a job in a restaurant washing dishes. Once you are in a restaurant, you will really get a feel for the job. Ask questions to all the cooks, especially the old ones. You may find it to crazy, or you may find just what you were expecting. Either way, this is the best way to do it. Most Chefs have started at the dish pit and moved on to the stove eventually.

My first job in a restaurant was in a pub washing morning and lunch dishes, sticky eggs and ketchup all over... I got so fast, that the Chef got me to help him making toast for clubhouse sandwiches, and soon after that it became my job to do the freakin' clubhouse, a lot of them and the dishes too! So, I left the pub and entered culinary school; that experience was the dealmaker for me! I felt part of something big. Do it, and I guarantee you won't regret it!

In 1986, just like today, you saw all kinds of people doing dishes in the food industry. There are people with a past that they are trying to forget, and people with a future they are trying to set up. No restaurant can function properly without a dishwashing team that gels, as they are the backbone of our industry, and I speak with knowledge because that's where I started. I can remember a young guy who came to me in my restaurant, asking for work. He was 17 years old, skinny and full of energy - the perfect combination! I hired him on the spot and told him he could start the next day. The following day, he showed up all keen, so my senior dishwashing teammate, an 18 year old kid, started to train him on how and where to put the dishes. I was actually out for a food run, so when I came back in the kitchen, I saw the new kid washing dishes... up to his elbow in the greasy water with the long sleeves of his shirt down, and both hands in the sink. I could not bring myself to say anything to him without cracking up laughing, so the entire evening I tried not to look in his direction, and on he went, with his sleeves down the whole night. The next day, he came in and the first thing he did was to roll up his sleeves… I figured that his mom must have had a conversation with him the night before! He stayed with us one and a half years, and no one ever brought up this subject.

Beware, heads up, watch out

The number one business for bankruptcies in America is still restaurants. Here is an interesting fact: nearly 50% of restaurants will fail within the first 3 years.

Heads up, in hotels, for example, you won't work side by side with the Executive Chef. So even if he is a top gun, it won't affect your learning that much, but it may give you a great reference. On the other hand, I have found that the right small restaurants can provide a great springboard for your career if they are combined with the right Chef.

Watch out - once you reach the level of head Chef, your schedule is going to be much easier to follow... you will work all the time (well, at least your mind will!)

A word of advice: Listen up... If one day your lawyer friend says you both should start a restaurant together, look at him/her in the eyes and just say no. Partnership is a great thing, but you need to make sure that both sides understand the workload involved. Two people from the industry have a better chance to succeed just based on the fact that they know the workload it takes to break even!

Beware: try to carry a back up Chef knife in your toolbox in the event that someone wants to borrow a knife. It is the best way to discourage them to ask for your knife again. Don't lend your good knives to anyone, EVER!

A word of advice: Don't date anyone from work, unless you can live with the fact that he/she may become your boss and/or better yet, become your worst enemy.

Watch out for the boss' best friend, as sometimes things can back fire in your direction!

Always ask for any promises management gives you in writing, especially if it's about money.

Safety first. Wear steel-toed shoes or clogs, as it is much safer for your pretty little toes!

Beware when the boss tells you things like; "You will get your raise soon." If this employer is serious about the quality of your work, your raise should be right away, and possibly even retroactive.

Heads up, promotions are usually given based on work performance, but not always. Make sure that you keep good and positive strategic alliances with your boss, and don't argue too much, as sometimes it may leave bad memories in his/her mind when promotion time comes around.

Heads up, if your boss gives you your pay cheque and asks you if you can wait until next week before cashing it in, beware! When money is tight in a restaurant, the first dollars made should go to employees. Some restaurateurs will try to con the employees into accepting a deal "just for this week", then one more week, then one more week, then you show up at work one day and it is locked up...and you need to look for another job.

A word of advice: Some Chefs may try to use the kitchen to create their own dictatorship. What I mean is, they will scream at you for every little mistake you make. In order to make it stop, just talk one-on-one with the Chef ASAP. Choose an office with the door closed and just say; "I don't treat you badly, so I deserve to be treated with respect. Nowhere on my resume does it say that I am perfect. This screaming at me is borderline harassment and I won't take it. I am here to learn my trade, and if you keep screaming at me I will leave." These type of Chefs are much more rare in today's kitchen than they were years ago, but you may still come across one or two during your career. Usually, but not always, after you speak to one of those Chefs, they tone down. In this case, the word "harassment" is a very powerful tool.

If you notice that many suppliers are calling every couple days to get paid, it is often a bad sign and the end may be closer than you think.

Beware: although it sometimes feels good, getting angry solves nothing! Deal with every issue as if you were talking to your mother or father… respect will get you to your goal. As a cook or a Chef, whenever possible, don't deal with issues while they are still hot. Wait instead until things cool down before bringing it up again. These tricks will often save your ass from being fired because you told the boss to piss off!

Heads up, many kitchens are still run the old fashioned way. The Chef may ask you to fetch his coffee, even if you don't drink coffee yourself. The last cook hired is often the one that will get the crappy jobs. In the old days, kitchens were run very much like the army.

In the newspaper, when you read "First cook/sous-Chef needed", it means, "We want a sous-Chef but will only pay first cook wage."

When you see "self starter needed" in the newspaper, it really means, "We want someone who has no personal life", because you will work many hours for a fixed salary.

If you notice that the same advertisement for a cook's position every couple months, there may be something wrong with the kitchen's management.

Beware: it is up to you, and not the employer, to keep your money straight. If an employer does not take off enough government taxes from your pay cheque each week, you may be left with having to pay Mr. or Mrs. Taxman a lump sum of money at the end of the year.

Private conversations between you and any coworker rarely stay just between the both of you.

Beware, if your Chef comes to you, shows you something odd looking and asks you, "Do you think this is OK?" the answer is no! If there were nothing wrong with this thing, he would not be asking you.

Once you start working, only show up 10 minutes ahead of time. Trust me, it's much harder to leave work on time, as often you will have to stay more than 8 hours.

Watch out - injuries happen quickly and often in the kitchen, so make sure you know where your first aid kit is located anywhere you work. It's not a bad idea to have a Level One first aid course under your belt before starting on your culinary path.

The fewer cooks there are in a kitchen, the harder it will be to take sick days. As a rule, unless you show up to work holding one of your bloody lungs in your hands, or missing a foot, you will be asked to come in to do your scheduled shift.

Beware of restaurants owned and operated by people without experience. This is a true story: I knew this guy who worked in a car assembly plant for 25 years. One day, he retired and opened up his dream restaurant. After the first invoice crossed his desk, he realized that good food was not cheap. So, he persuaded the Chef at the time that boar was way too expensive and they should just buy pork and keep the expensive printed menu the way it was. Then came the lobster... he told every waiter that if a customer asked for the lobster plate, they were to say, the lobster was not very good quality at the market this morning, so it's unfortunately unavailable tonight. He never bought lobster again, and it took 7 months before he re-printed the menu, but only two months before his Chef left him.

Watch out for restaurants that change Chef every 4 months; it may not be the best place to work after all!

<u>A word of advice:</u> even if you have, or think you have a close relationship with someone at work, it does not mean that you are immune against harassment lawsuits. Although it is one of the most popular subjects in professional kitchens, sexual jokes and/or simple comments can cause you serious trouble. Trust me on this - always use proper etiquette when you talk to your coworkers, bosses or customers. Harassment complaints can really put a stop to your career progress.

Heads up, fires do happen in the kitchen, so have preventive measures in place and/or a plan to evacuate in a hurry.

Heads up - fridges are supposed to be cold, so keep your eyes open, you never know when they're going to break. Trust me, they will break, especially around spring and fall when the temperature changes.

Watch out - cooks steal each other's mise-en-place all the time. Be especially careful of the one that tells you, "No, it's not me!" So use your survival skills, and hide your precious stuff anywhere you can.

Safety first. Always think about what can go wrong before you start something, and always adjust your work accordingly for your safety and others. You only get one body for about 80 years, so take care of yourself.

Beware: lock your tools if you want to be able to use them the next day. Shit will disappear, especially tongs, hand towels and cookbooks. Oh and they rarely come back. So, engrave your initials on everything.

Watch out - if you want credit for your new ideas, bring them to the Chef yourself, or someone else will do it for you.

Beware: always, always learn everything there is to know about a machine before starting to work on it. It only takes half a second to lose a thumb, and a lifetime of hardship to eat burgers without a thumb on your best hand.

Heads up - always attend all the company picnics or events, as it really shows your interest in being part of the team. Promotions are often just around the corner.

Watch out - If the Chef asked you to do something, get on it promptly. I have seen many cooks get chewed up because they did not comply fast enough. Keep in mind this is not like when Papa asks you to do something. You cannot negotiate with the Chef, so just do it.

A word of advice: Creating relationships between coworkers is extremely important, so take the time to sit down once in a while and get to know the people that you work with you. Promotions don't just happen because you do a good job; sometimes, it helps to know people.

Can I speak to the Chef?

Once you are the Chef, everyone will want to speak to you about his or her cats, dogs or uncles, carrots or even dead lobsters in the fridge. You will need to find answers if at all possible...

A word of advice: Don't make decisions without thinking about the consequences. You are better off to tell someone, "Let me think about this" than to end up putting your foot in your mouth in front of everyone else. No one has all the answers, not even the Chef. But, in the kitchen you are the one that has to make the decision if no one else can. If the captain of the ship can't decide, it does not instill much confidence in the crew. The secret to a successful team is when everyone can follow your example and gain their own confidence.

To limit the amount of questions you get in a day, train your crew to make decisions by themselves; it will pay off.

In the early nineties, I worked in a bakery inside a grocery store near Montreal. I was the head baker, supervisor and manager - I was it! We did Danish, breads, buns, croissants, pizzas, muffins... the works. My crew was made of highly experienced, unionized cashiers who did not want to work the cash station anymore. So, I had to do some major training to get them to understand the basics of defrosting dough, baking and ordering. OK, so 99% of the bread dough products came to us frozen in boxes, and all we needed to do was open the box, proof and/or defrost the dough and bake it. Simple enough, you would think. So, I explained to them over and over again how to see if your bread is ready to take out of the oven. But really, the cooking times for this dough were so regular that cooking time would vary by less than 3 minutes. Every week, part of my job was to give out this report to my boss. I would have to go in the office on the second floor on the other side of the building to use the computer and do my inventory count. Seven and a half months after we started working together, I am in the office and I get this stupid phone call, "Hey Martin, is the bread ready to come out of the oven?" It was in French, but my answer was still a touch abrupt: "Why the "beep" are you asking me, you are standing in front of the oven, looking at the loaves inside, and I am way the hell far away, at the back in the office. Do you think you could take a chance and take it out? You have been working in this department for 7½ months, and you still don't know if the bread is ready when the buzzer goes off..." I left shortly after that due to work-rage illness; I just did not want to kill someone! They were nice ladies and all, but they were just not born bakers!

You should have an open door policy and an open mind attitude. If you always seriously consider any new ideas, you will always be ahead of the competition. Innovation is the key to longevity in the kitchen, and your cooks are full of untapped ideas.

If you want to really make a positive impact on your team of cooks, you should cook a simple meal for them. If they are given a chance to sit down at a table and talk to you about life and other subjects besides work, they will really appreciate it.

A word of advice: Always give clear directions to get clear results. You have to have a plan, and it needs to be clear before you share it with your cooks. Indecision drives people crazy!

Not all, but most people, want to do good work, so make sure that you give great support to your cooks and they will make you look good in return.

Set deadlines for your supervisors, and make sure that you check on them before they reach it. It is your job to help them become better at what they do.

Empower your cooks to take calculated decisions; it will make them feel like they belong on the team. No one wants to be the bench warmer... I have to tell you this one: in 1999, I accepted a management position near our house. Basically, I was hoping that it would allow me to be more available at home. It was a small neighborhood eatery/pub that made sandwiches, soups and chili. I was the manager, making sure that operations ran smoothly and that labour cost and food cost were on track. After almost one year, my team and I had managed to improve sales and be more cost efficient. At this point, all we were talking about in those days was how much we needed more sales, and how great it was when we were busy.

One night, I was at a Christmas party across town enjoying myself and forgetting about works, yes, even drinking!

After I had just finished my first 3 beers, my pager rang, so I picked up my message to find out that it was one of my supervisors, asking me to call him back right away. I picked up the nearest phone and called him back. He answered, and I said, " It's Martin, " and he said, " Martin, we're on fire! " Now with my very limited French speaking abilities, combined with my 3 beers, I said " Wow that's great, how busy are we? " He said, " No really, we're on fire, the oven is burning down! " Again, partially tipsy, I said, "What the beep are you calling me for, call 911!" and I started laughing uncontrollably! He then started to explain to me that he had called 911and the owner of the business, and everything was under control. It was the funniest phone call I ever got from work.

<u>**A word of advice:**</u> **if you only remember this out of the whole book, it's worth it.** *"As a Chef, if your kitchen does not make a profit at the end of the year, your job is in jeopardy."*

You absolutely need to structure your menu so it generates profits, and the more the better! Know your numbers - your job depends on it. Think about it: if the kitchen does not make profits, why the hell do they need you?

The computer is your friend - learn to use it to your advantage to save time and money. It may take you a few hours to set up a schedule format that works, but it saves huge time in the long run. The less paper work you have, the better.

Quality, quality and quality... if you create menu items, keep your cost in mind, but do not sacrifice quality for price point. Today's customers are knowledgeable enough to know if you give them poor quality food. Adjust your price according to your menu, not the other way around.

Don't spend too much time in your office, and do regular check-up walks anytime you can. The more you are visible, the better your team will respect you. Talk and listen to your cooks; communication is everything.

Be a teacher! Any Chef that takes the time to show his cooks something new will keep them much longer. If they keep learning, why would they go anywhere else? Reducing staff turnover is very important if you don't want to have to hire new cooks every other day.

Watch the garbage cans in your kitchen on a regular basis. It will make the cooks pay more attention to what they throw away, and it will improve profit.

Time management will become essential once you are the Chef. Plan your days very carefully and allow space for unexpected crap... You can use any electronic gismo available to you to make sure that your time is well spent. Stay away from micro-managing your cooks; instead, make better use of your supervisors, by doing daily speed meeting each morning.

The best tool you have to improve the performance in your kitchen is your cook's schedule. Most people if they had to choose, would choose a better schedule over money. Giving an unexpected day off, whether it is paid or not, will always make a cook feel good. Flexibility and creativity with the schedule is a great way for you to reward your team, but just make sure it's done fairly.

A word of advice: Don't be a screamer. The more you scream, the less they produce once you're gone... it's basic human behavior.

Suggestions coming from the cooks on the front line are priceless. Listen and write things down, as you never know when you may need that idea!

Once you have a behavior problem with a cook on your team, it is extremely important that you take care of it as fast as you can. The rest of your team is counting on you to fix the bad apple or get rid of it. If you do nothing for too long, you will be seen as weak and unreliable.

Follow up is extremely important. If your cooks know that you will check back on their work, their performance will be better. On the other hand, if they know you never follow up, they will slack off; it's basic human behavior.

When you make promises, keep them. There is nothing worst than a Chef who says yes but doesn't come through. Your word should be gold!

Think of perks that you can supply to your staff… I worked at this place years ago, and every December, the owners would give me a slab of frozen smoked salmon as a Christmas gift. It sure helps me like him a bit more.

Even if the company has a reward program for employees of the month, create a CHEF kitchen award that is given to an outstanding cook once a month. Allow yourself be influenced by your cooks, as they will always be more critical of themselves then you would. In the past, I used a steel bowl. I had a plaque engraved once a month with the cook's name. It became a prized possession among the team members. Your cooks look up to you, it will mean a lot to them if you do this, and ultimately you will benefit from a highly motivated team.

Don't be shy to tell your cooks how much you like their work, and watch them the rest of the day as they perform even better than normal.

Teach yourself to go out in the dining room to meet your customers as often as you can. This kind of public relations is the best tool for return business. People love to see the Chef, and it makes the meal even more special when you can ask questions to the Chef about each dish.

At one point, I asked Chloae to tell me exactly why she wants to be a Chef. Her answer was simple, she said, "Papa, I want to learn to make spaghetti and meat balls the way you do." So I said, "Well, you don't have to be Chef for that, I can show you myself." She answered, That's great, but I still want to be a Chef." So, I said to her, "Well, why do you want to be a Chef?" and she said, "I want to go to school and learn about cakes, pies, roasts beef and chocolate." Ok, now it makes more sense, I thought. If you become a Chef, you will do all those things and more. So, you can go back to reading...

Ultimately, the customer signs your pay cheques, so keep in mind that customer service is extremely important. Don't be shy to go all out to give a little extra. The best example, I have is this: in 2003, my team and I cooked a luncheon for 35 people. They were all staying at the hotel for the weekend to attend a wedding. Everything went smoothly, the food was great and the service was perfect. After lunch, the bride came to me with a question. It should have been simple, but no way, not that day! She asked me if I could get the leftovers of her wedding cake from the day before. She said, "I gave it to this guy yesterday, and he said it would be in THE fridge." The only problem was that in our hotel, we had something like 40-50 different fridges spread over 9 floors in 8 different kitchens. I told her that she could go back to her table while I was searching for it, and that I would bring it to her once I had located the cake. I started to make some calls to all the departments, asking for her cake - starting with the bell desk, where often packages like these would end up. I finally spoke to some girl in Pastry who said, "Yes, I've got it, it's right here in my fridge!" I hung up the phone and I ran up 3 floors to the pastry shop to find out that this girl "thought" it was here, but did not really have it. After giving her a piece of my mind, I ran down one floor to check some other fridges in our main kitchen, but I found nothing... I ran back down to the first floor to go talk to the lady and try ask her a few more questions, hoping that she could remember who took the cake. I got to the private dining room where she was supposed to be, and she was gone... I then ran to the front desk and asked if I could find out which room number they had at the hotel. I did get the room number (they were in the Honeymoon Suite) but I still didn't have the freakin' wedding cake leftovers! Suddenly, it hit me! I ran up 4 floors to the room service department and sure enough, the cake was there. I grabbed it and ran up to the Honeymoon Suite on the 9th floor. I get there, and realize that I have to go up two more flights of stairs to reach their room. I get there only to find the maid cleaning the room. I ask her if she knew if the couple had left the building and she did not know, so I called down to the bell desk and the guy answering said that the bride and groom had just checked out 15 minutes ago... I decided to take one last chance, so I ran down two flights of stairs, 9 floors, then across the hotel into the lobby…I walk outside and bam! I saw the bride getting into her car, so I extended the cake box to her and said, "Have a great life!" This 45 minutes of my life was filled with frustration and stress, but added up to great customer service…and that bride had no idea!

PART THREE
THE BREAD

Job search

The second half of this book is about possible Chef jobs. I have rounded up for you a good selection of possibilities based on information gathered over the years, listening to cooks and Chefs around me. My personal experiences will also be a factor in some cases, as I have worked in many of those options presented here. Depending on concept, food, schedule, money or fringe benefits, this will give you a quick look into many different Chef opportunities that may be presented to you once you have completed culinary school.

You should be able to find a position that fits in with your desire, personality, skills, and lifestyle choice.

Searching in the newspapers at the beginning of your career is OK, but as you progress on this culinary path, you will need to broaden your search on the Internet and even probably use agencies that search for the perfect position for you. Always keep your eyes open and your ears to the ground, as in our industry everyone knows about everyone's business. The best place you can find out about new opportunities is at work. Keep in mind that a restaurant closing down is often the place where a new restaurant will reopen soon. Make sure you stay in touch with as many cooks and Chefs as you can, and that way work will find you instead of you finding it.

When all is said and done, in certain jobs, you may live a totally different experience than what I lived. All I can tell you is what these places are like in general, and hope that you can make your own decisions. Personally, some of these jobs I discovered 10 years too late in my career, and so I would have loved to have this information much earlier.

Cooking is a great profession; it will allow you to meet people from every corner of the world often without having to travel very far away. Once you have decided to take the culinarian path, you should seek an employer that will make you grow as a person and as a cook. At anytime during the first ten years, if you are no longer learning, you should move on, unless the particular job you are in turns out to be the perfect job for you.

Ask your next employer

At this stage, I want to take a few pages to give you a few pointers about getting through the hiring process without too much trouble.

When you go for an interview, show up 10 minutes ahead of time, but you might also plan to get to the parking lot 20 minutes ahead, just to make sure you are not late for your first impression. You can dress up for the occasion, but you don't need to go all out - clean and presentable is fine. Remove any visible body piercing for the interview, and once you have the job you may well be OK. Sit straight, don't slouch and don't chew gum. Shake hands with everyone present, no exceptions.

A word of advice: Don't ever light a cigarette or ask to light one during an interview, even if everybody else is smoking. If someone offers you one, just say "No thanks, not right now"!

Usually, I don't bother talking about money until I know that I want to work there. If you find out that this is not a place that fits with your career goals, it should not really matter how much money they are willing to pay you. There are some times in your life when necessity makes you take on positions driven by money. However, I can tell you from experience that if you don't really want to work there now, you probably won't change your mind later.

A word of advice: You should have done some research about the place before the interview, and you should be able to explain in 3 minutes or less why your past experience would fit well with what they are looking for in the position. If you don't know why you want to work somewhere, it will show up in the interview, and you may not get the job.

It is perfectly acceptable to ask questions to a potential employer, as it will show that you know what you want and you will be perceived as very professional.

A word of advice: Always wait until the end before you ask too many questions. Many times the employer will answer some of your questions during the interview process.

Listen very carefully to everything the employer will tell you, and take notes if necessary (it's OK, they will respect that).

Find your own words to ask your questions, as you don't want to sound like a telegram.

Look in the staff parking lot and try to see if, in general, the staff all drive old beat up cars or nice newer ones. It may help you see how much money this employer pays or doesn't pay his staff.

Why did the last person leave? This may flash some light onto why they are looking. At the very least, it will show you how much the employer is willing to tell you. I am always on the defense when they refuse to tell me why!

What kind of training do I get will show you if this employer takes pride in setting you up for success. No matter how much experience you may have when you start a new position in a kitchen, serious employers should always give you some training to show you around. You should be matched up with a more senior cook in that kitchen and get at the very least the 5 minute tour of the fridges, dry storage, your work station, your daily routine, and introduce you to all coworkers present at the time.

What kind of opportunity do they have for you once you have master this position? This is always a great thing to know. Some employers will expect you to do the same functions forever, and others will have a clear plan of where they would like you to go next! Ultimately, the ideal situation is for your career goals to be a good match with their future plans.

What are my daily duties? This is definitely a good question, because it is a way to avoid unpleasant surprises. Ask about the work you will actually do - it can possibly make or break the deal if it's a really boring job.

What is my schedule? Here is another good one, a well-managed kitchen will have a data bank of part-time cooks that can be called when you are sick or if someone died, not me, but someone else!

What about sick days? You should find out ahead of time what happen if you are sick. How many paid sick days do they allow?

Can we talk about benefits... This one is to avoid surprises; why not ask right now, before your next wisdom tooth starts aching again. Benefits vary from one restaurant to the next, as they do with hotels, summer camps, etc.

What about meals? I know, it sounds stupid being a cook or a Chef working in a kitchen, but in many places, the staff has to pay for all meals taken from the kitchen, I'm just saying, ask before to avoid surprises. In many cases, the employer will take a fixed amount off your pay cheque every week, whether you eat or not.

When do you allow holiday time? It may seem like a stupid question but trust me, it's not! Think about it: you don't want to find out right before your next annual surfing trip that you can't have holidays during that time. It is common in this industry to black out business peak times for holidays. Well, guess what? Some of those restaurants will peak year around.

The choices

This is it Chloae, this is the meat of the book. I have put a list together of potential jobs that you can seek as a cook and/or Chef. It is a general overview, but I cover 39 of the most common places where you can be a cook and/or a chef. This section should help you figure out where you would want to work. Take your time, and write down the places that look like potential options for you. Then, search for more information on the Internet, Yellow Pages, library and newspapers about the specific details on those choices. You could also call and go to the actual restaurant and talk to people working there. Remember, you need to put as much time searching for a culinary job as you do buying a pair of shoes.

The French Restaurants are still to this day the backbone of our industry for trends and upcoming Chefs. Often, these restaurants will serve new interpretations and/or classic dishes. Many of these restaurants are a high-end type concept with plenty of hoop-la to blow your mind. The kitchen is usually modern with all the essential equipment. Yet, I have seen some of these kitchens without a deep fryer in place. The kitchen crew can be 3 cooks minimum up to 20 or 30.

The schedule here is designed to accommodate lunch and dinner service. You may work something like 7am to 3pm, or 3pm to 11pm. either way, you should get two days off in a row, but not always. You should definitely expect to do overtime. Money is OK most of the time, to good in some rare cases. If you own the place, you may manage to make a few more dollars at the end of the year.

When I owned my French restaurant, I was 20 years old and full of energy. We prided ourselves on the fact that we never ran out of anything for our customers. Well, one night, we got an order for our famous kiwi tartlets and found out that we were out of kiwi for the topping. I jumped in my car to go get some at the local grocery store. Montreal in December: it was a freezing evening, so I turned the heating fan to maximum to try to generate some heat fast! I got to the store and ran inside, screaming "Kiwi!" as I was going through the door. The store clerk - who knew us very well - said "Next to the bananas", so I grabbed 4 kiwis and said "Put it on our account" as I ran outside. I got to my car and yes, you've guessed it, I had left the engine running with the fan full blast and the door locked. All I could think of was, "My customer is waiting for her dessert!" so I ran up the hill - in minus18C with only my skimpy Chef jacket. I got to the restaurant very cold, walked in out of breath and said, "stupid kiwi tartlet, we have to take them off the menu if she only knew."

Overall, the French restaurant is a great place to learn the culinary art at a classic level.

The ethnic restaurants can be challenging, but also an amazing place to really learn the authentic way of doing Indian food, Greek or Italian, Thai or Chinese... My best friend used to work in a gastronomic Italian restaurant while he was at school, and to this day he still remembers how to make a great Italian feast. He used to tell us that he could barely understand the Chef's directions through the very thick Tuscan accent, but he sure would know when the Chef was mad.

Schedules vary from place to place, and money can be OK to good. I can just imagine you, Chloae, in a Chinese or Mexican restaurant, learning all their secret recipes and a few words at the same time. If you ever have a chance to do an internship in an ethnic restaurant, choose right and it will look great on your resume.

The five diamond restaurants are the "Michael Jordan's" of all restaurants. They are the best in the business, the finest food, unbelievable service, the most convoluted and yes, also the most expensive. The entire restaurant will have an amazing number of servers and cooks, and also will have on staff a great sommelier, one or two bartenders and a few hosts. The owner will have lots of money invested into the place, and stress will be pretty high everyday.

Five-diamond status does not happen by wishful thinking; the owner will have invested time and money to reach that level. For example: In a good quality 40 seat French restaurant, you can expect the crew to be around 5 cooks and 5 servers. In a five diamond place, you will most likely have 9-14 cooks and about the same number of serving staff. The idea is simple: the customer must have a perfect experience every time, no excuses. When you have plenty of people to do the job, it makes things much easier to impress the customers. The food is done from scratch, and everything must be done fresh daily. From the ice cream to the whipped butter to the sauces to the breads, everything has to be fresh, no excuses. The menu will reflect the most current trends and a strong influence from the world's market.

The more the restaurant is famous, the more a job here may be hard to get, as many people want to work in these places. The interview process should be fairly rigorous, and so having good references will help you a lot.

Once you start cooking at one of these places -and I hope you do, as it is a great experience to have on your resume - you will be in the midst of creativity at its best.

A word of advice: shut up, look around, listen and learn!

These places will usually work nights, and have only one schedule for everyone: if it's open, the whole team is on! Everyone will often have the same days off, and the same holidays, as it often closes for only a few weeks every year.

The money should be good. You will see and learn great work, but you will also have to be able to deal with the stress in the kitchen. The products that you will use in the kitchen will be the finest in the world. You should be able to work with fresh truffles on a regular basis and caviar in profusion. If I have one regret with my culinary career, it is that I never directly worked in a five-diamond restaurant. I really hope that you do!

The small bistro is usually located in an urban neighborhood. The regular customers are people who like to go out and sit at a table, talking over the day with friends, or reading a book while munching on simple dishes. The menus are tapas-like, but often a touch cheaper in price and quality. Wholesome food with flair is the norm, and there is usually only a very small kitchen in which to work your magic. The crew is made of 2 or 3, including the Chef. The schedule is a normal lunch and dinner structure with sometime breakfast, and money is not so good to good, due to the fact that it's a small place. Often owned and operated by the Chef, this can be a great place to work while you are at culinary school with still lots to learn.

The breakfast and brunch restaurants are great if you want to be home at night. These concepts are more and more popular. They offer breakfast and lunch only during the week and brunch on the weekend. As a cook, it limits your culinary growth because you will be learning only the range of food for these meals. The schedule is something like 5, 6 or 7 am to 1, 2 or 3 pm, allowing you to have a second jobs at night if you wish. The money is a drawback, as most breakfast menus do not generate big sales and so your pay cheque will usually reflect that. You can expect not so good to good money maximum. I am very happy that some cooks do choose the breakfast shift, because your grand father and I went out for breakfast together every time we could! After a while working in one of those places, no one will be able to say of you, "She can't even fry an egg."

The 24-hour restaurants create busy kitchens. Imagine this: you never stop cooking, ever! These concepts can cause certain problems in the kitchen. One major problem is the fridges. Your prep-work for the next day may be used up by the time you show up for your next shift. Also, you had better be good at making things like eggs and French toast during dinner hours, because these items are often on the all day menu. The schedule needs to have a minimum of one cook on shift at all time, especially if it is a unionized kitchen as the waiters can't touch any food. Graveyard shifts can be lots of fun if you like to work alone. The money is not so good to OK, and may be good in some cases if you are the head Chef. Benefits should be good, but don't expect great culinary discoveries in one of those places. Twenty-four hour restaurants are great to learn to be a better line cook, as it will usually get busy at some point during the day. They may also be a great place to have a simple job while you make other plans - like looking for a husband or having grandchildren.

The Tapas restaurants have gained a lot of popularity in the last 5 years. I like this concept a lot, because it allows me as a customer to taste many dishes in one night out. From the cook's point of view, if you have a Chef that likes to keep it fresh and create new ideas on a regular basis, this could be a great place to work. This type of concept may allow you to explore your creativity everyday. If you find a Chef that keeps you challenged, this is a great place to learn valuable skills. Many times, these places are non-union and operate in a small kitchen, but often in an open concept design that lets you see the customers, which can be very nice.

Your schedule is going to be lunch and/or dinner service, as many of these places are open later at night. The money can be OK to good, depending on how successful the particular restaurant is.

The employee's cafeterias around the world have one thing in common: they have to feed employees that may or may not necessarily be happy at their jobs. You will be asked to make creative, wonderful and flavorful meals with a very strict budget. You will have to use, use and re-use all leftovers you can to bring your food cost down. Your menu will be simple and the choices very limited, and you will see the same customer faces day in and day out. When you make chicken, some customers will ask for fish, and yes, when you make fish, some customers will ask for the chicken. Some of the jobs can be unionized. Oh, and you will have to learn to make a killer meatloaf! The money is not so great to OK, but often these jobs are very secure, as the company will always need someone to cook. The schedule is usually great: you would work something like 6am-2pm or 7 -3, leaving you to be home with your family at night.

When I left the fine dining world in 1989, first I needed a holiday, and then I needed a job. I called my best friend Yves, and asked for a simple, low stress, fun job... He said, "Come and work for me, it's going to be fun!" And so I did! It was at a General Motors auto-part supplier, a cafeteria serving 250 unionized workers 2 meals a day. I had never worked in a low-key kitchen; it was a great education and yes, it was lots of fun working with my best pal. Lasagnas, ragout, Shepherd's pie, brownies and ice cream… it was the perfect place to forget about the stress of working in a fine dining restaurant. I can recall an interesting client, one that would complain about the 45-cent cup of coffee being too expensive and not good enough. Everyday, day in, day out for the whole year I was there, and he kept saying, "It's too expensive" or "It's bad coffee". One day I reached the limit of my patience, so as he started his same daily routine about the price and quality of our coffee, I just lost it on him. I started to tell him that I had calculated that he was drinking 9 cups a day, so the quality couldn't be that bad, and that at 9 cups a day it does make it a touch expensive. I went on to tell him that after 17 years at the same job, he was a bitter man. I then continued by telling him that he had been working at this job for way too long and he needed to find a job that could make him happy, because there was not a cup of coffee in this world that could do that for him. I closed by telling him that he could always bring his own coffee thermos and stop bothering us. I then turned around and went back to my burgers and French fries… Whichever career <u>you</u> choose, don't be a bitter woman doing it - just find something else.

The school cafeterias are very similar to the employee cafeterias, except you will deal with challenging young kids - the leaders of tomorrow that have not developed a sense of respect for others yet. You may even have to help them yourself become more respectful human beings. The meals are usually supervised by a dietician (government), so that will create challenges for your menu, but it is a good thing to have someone watch over our kids' food. The money is similar to other cafeterias, not so good to ok, in some cases it will be unionized, helping a bit for salaries. The schedule is usually great. You would work something like 6am-2pm or 7 -3, leaving you to be home with your family every night. What are the big advantages of school? You've guessed it – long summer holidays are a sure thing…

The hospital is a unique work experience, highly supervised and generally unionized. Hospitals have the responsibility of making people feel better, yet it is a well-known fact that the taste of the food has nothing to do with that process. Example, cardiac patients who have always eaten salty food and find themselves laying in a hospital bed one day, eating a pasty white chicken breast with plain rice and vegetables, without any salt on it… well, bland is the word that comes to mind.

As a professional cook, you will need

to learn certain skills to work in this industry. First, you will have to accept the fact that your food may not taste just the way you want. Instead, it tastes the way you have to make it to keep your job. These positions are usually not creative based, but very structured, so you had better follow the recipes until you leave this job. These are very good places to learn to cook special diets for people.

The schedules are based on a kitchen that serves 3 meals a day, but you will most likely only work 8-hour shifts with 2 days off in a row per week. OK money to start and regular small increases after that!

The corporate Chef type of position is a mixture of Public Relations and kitchen Guru! You often work alone or with a small team, and usually in a state of the art kitchen. Your role will be to create standard recipes and menus for the corporation. You will also create training manuals, do some sourcing of products and attend media events, just to name a few. Money is great to amazing and the schedule is also nice, like 9am – 5pm Monday to Friday. This is the type of job you can reach after a few years of experience.

The specialty restaurants - pizza, pasta, and steakhouses - will be in every town that you come across. Menus are built for large numbers, and seating is in a nice but casual dining room. It's not rare (no pun intended) to see 400 or more covers (people served) for a single dinner in a steakhouse. The kitchen is big and efficient, and timing is everything, as a steak can't wait 5 minutes under the pass. Once the order is up, away it goes. The servers usually have lots of experience and do an incredible job keeping up with the kitchen. If you find out that you like routine work, then this is a great place for you. Menus don't change a whole lot, and neither should your schedule. Lunch or dinner, good steakhouses will keep you busy. Money is not so good to ok, but if you are in charge you could reach good.

When you talk about a nice wood-burning oven **pizza restaurant or an Italian pasta restaurant**, keep in mind that you will usually do the same job and work on the same menu for many years. I have found that these positions are great to really learn to get good at one thing - if you do the same task everyday you will get good at it! Also, these concepts can be a great place to use as a springboard to a management position. It's much easier to manage a small crew with a small menu for your first management job.

The private Chef would follow one person or even a whole family, and cook for them wherever they go! These jobs can be very exciting, depending on who is your employer. Mostly, it is wealthy families, government officials, famous stars or corporate professionals that can afford a private Chef. Traveling and entertaining is usually a big part of their life. If we say you would normally cook for a family of 4 people, it is not impossible that one weekend you would end up coordinating a dinner for 100 or more of their closest friends!

Schedules in these jobs are very simple: you are almost always on shift. You get some personal time, but having to cook 3 meals a day can cramp your style a bit! Money is good to great to amazing in some cases. They would most likely provide you with things like accommodation and access to a car, with or without a chauffer. The details of these jobs are very custom-made to the life style of the people you cook for on a daily basis. You may have to travel in ugly places like Grand Cayman or Hawaii, or you may also end up in Africa, London or Paris, so although hectic, the benefits are not too bad!

The personal Chef will basically go to people's homes and cook for them. It could be cooking for a private party, giving private cooking classes or cooking multiple meals for people looking for another option instead of always eating out. The schedule is flexible according to the customer's needs. The money is ok to good once you are well established, but the flexibility to work other projects (like writing a book) can help with your income. This is what papa is doing now, and I love it. It allows me to work on different menus every time, work in different kitchens every time, and meet new people every time. I have found my calling after 20 years; I can work on many projects, be my own boss and still make an OK living.

The fishing boat can be a lot of fun. You will cook for 4 – 12 fishermen that work hard and eat a lot. The good thing is that you will have access to fresh fish. The bad thing is that you will smell like fish when you come back home, which is not necessarily a big advantage if you are trying to meet a husband that will give me grandchildren! The food is homemade style dishes with big portions for big appetites. The ocean and/or the fishes will dictate the schedule. Overall, when the season starts, you work until it ends. In the off-season, you can stay home and play in the snow, as there is not much fishing happening in the winter. Money is good to great while you work. Many people born and raised near the ocean will choose this kind of cooking job.

The cruise ship kitchen is mostly a man's world, with few exceptions. You could be the exception, Chloae, but before you go sign up, I should explain to you why not many women work in these kitchens. Imagine this, you are the only woman in a kitchen of 70 plus men who work a 365-day contract without their wives. Yes you can do it, but it would be very hard emotionally. Your work contract would usually last 2 to 6 months, and you would start working around 6 hours after you get on board. You would probably stop working around 10 hours before the end of your contract when you get off the ship.

Your schedule will be 11-12 hours of work a day, 7 days a week. Now wait, you won't do 12 in a row, you will usually work from 6 am until 10:30 pm with flexible breaks in between. You should get 2 hours off in the afternoon, and you can sleep it off or you can go on shore to visit the world... The life on board can be a bit cramped and make you feel claustrophobic, but like everything else you should be able to get use to it. The party scene is great, the booze is cheap and you will meet people from around the world. No matter how much experience on land you may have at the time, your first shift in the kitchen will be reminiscent of one of the great battle scenes from the Lord of the Ring movies. It busy, it's loud and it's Chaos. The good news is that you do get used to it, but everything you have learned so far may not be enough. Money is great, partially because you don't really spend that much. They pay for your meals, room, laundry and medical while on board; they also pay to fly you to the ship and back. So in theory it is the perfect job, but you will need to get used to it. I saw a cook work 48 hours before getting fired. He could not work and have a social life the way he did on land, his first and second day he showed up drunk and that was it! But there were other cooks who had done it for years, without many days off.

The guests come from all over, and they often, I mean really often, ask stupid questions. I can recall being in the middle of the ocean doing circles north of Cuba, and this guest stops me to ask does the crew sleep on board? We were in hurricane season with one in front and one behind us, and this lady asks me why the ship is moving? My favorite was this old man standing in front of our Sushi bar about to order, and said to my cook, "Is this Guacamole?"

Just keep in mind that these jobs will give you a chance to see the world and make good money, but it is very hard on the people that you may leave behind, like your old papa.

The wineries can provide a great place to work. You would obviously have to move to wine country somewhere, but there are worse places to live in this world. The customers that visit these places will either be foodies or wine aficionados. Most of the time, the food served in these kitchens is refreshing, fun and, of course, perfectly matched with the wine. It would be a great asset for your career to learn the art of wine and food pairing. Your schedule is going to be dictated by the wine itself, because in some cases you will be laid off during the non-growing season. You should have regular days off, but no holiday time allowed during peak business season. Money should be OK to good, and when you reach the executive winery Chef status, money will be great to amazing. These wineries can really help you learn the art of cooking, and give you the experience necessary to become a great Chef.

The truck stop will create job security for you. If you do a good job, you can retire in these places. Think about it - when was the last time you saw one of these concepts close down? The schedule will match the 24-hour format of the truck stop: breakfast, lunch, dinner or graveyard. The money is not so good to good, but you can eat all the French fries you want... When I travel by car, I make a point of stopping in these establishments to eat a steak or burger. No major culinary discoveries are made there, but they do have awesome burgers!

The restaurant chains make for a large part of the casual dining scene in America. Depending on the concept, the food should be OK. Whether it's Italian, Greek or Mexican, you will learn. The main thing to remember is that you won't create menus or recipes in these places. The corporate Chef takes care of all creations. You will however learn to be a great line cook and possibly learn some great management skills if given the opportunity. These kitchens are often unionized. The schedule will be lunch or dinner, and you should get two days off per week. The money is not so good to good. Many of these concepts will have open design kitchens that let people see you at work. These places can be a great springboard before going to culinary school.

The bars and pubs will let you practice your deep-frying arm. Again, with some exceptions, bar and pub kitchens will serve lots of deep fried food and have very limited menus. Some places will put the emphasis on comfort food, but still, there is usually no major culinary discovery here. Schedule can be lunch, dinner or later. The money is not so good to good if you are the Chef in charge of everything. The great advantage is that you will save on driving, as you are already at the pub after work. Don't drink and drive.

The private caterers change location every day. Be prepared to learn to troubleshoot as much as you will learn to cook. I have lots of respect for cooks and Chefs that cater on location. This is not an easy task, as if you forget to bring something, you cannot always go get it. Equipment breaks down in a normal use, but if you start carrying it around in a van, it will break constantly and without warning. Almost every time you transport food in a van, things fall down, shit will happen, for sure!

The schedule is flexible around the events like many other catering type jobs. The money goes from not so good to great once you make it into the big league catering companies. The food is usually exceptionally fresh as it is made to specification for each event. If you are the type who would like to do bungee jumping, scuba diving or ice climbing this may just be for you. It can be fun! When my wife and I were doing catering, we did a private party at Tim Robbins and Susan Sarandon's house. I still remember the smell! We had a great plan, nine whole smoked chickens was the main course. That morning, everything was on schedule, until our truck decided not to start. Our BBQ trailer was usually attached to that truck, so we then had to smoke the chickens inside our truck like boy scouts. So I did - I started a fire at the bottom of my oven, and placed my chickens inside the oven until done... 3 ½ hours to be exact! About half way into our adventure, Tim Robbins came to the back door of the mobile kitchen to ask if everything was all right. We both looked at him and said, "Sure, everything is fine." The smoke was so thick that we were both crying! The party went smoothly though, and we had fun too.

Movie catering is the second most demanding job I ever did. If you can't get up early in the morning, if you like routine work, if you are not a disciplined person or if you can't avoid peeing for 12 hours, this job is definitely not for you. On a movie set, life is simple: the philosophy is "get it done" no matter what. You have to be on time, all the time. If the meal is late, you can kiss your big-buck job good bye... The producer rules, so if he wants breakfast on one side of town and lunch on the other side of town, well you need to get it done. A big part of your day will be trouble shooting just like on the Canteen truck, but no matter what, don't be late. You will have your full kitchen inside your truck, and be asked to serve creative, tasty and well balanced meals. Your menu will be simple but extensive for breakfast, and lunch changes everyday.

A normal crew would be around 100-140 people, and some days you will also have to feed extras ... from 1 to a few hundred extra people. The location will change constantly and when you go to bed, you may not always know what time you start working the next day. You would receive a phone call in the middle of the night telling you at what time the superstars wanted to eat breakfast.

Money is great, and you earn every dollar of it... Schedule is normally Monday to Friday, 70-80 hours of work! Usually Saturday you sleep, and Sunday you take care of house stuff (laundry, paying the bills, etc.) and see your family. So many things can go wrong when you cook inside a truck. Watch out for flat tires, because that can really screw up your day no matter how good the stew tastes that day...

On a certain December 19, the last day of work before Christmas, I was preparing to cook a marvelous dinner for a TV series crew of 120 people. The menu was "surf & turf" - T-bone and Steamed King Crab. I cooked breakfast without any problems, I made my soup, my vegetables were pre-cooked that day, the crab was ready to go, and the grill was hot and ready to receive the T-bones. Now, you need to know that the day before, I cooked Fish & Chips and used up way more propane that I thought! Thirty-five minutes before game time, I was just starting to mark my steaks when the propane went dead... I looked up everywhere and realized quickly that it was empty. I stormed out of the truck, ran all the way to the special effects people, to ask to borrow one of their propane tanks. I was saved! No, not yet - my boss had removed from my truck the adaptor necessary to transfer the propane from the tank to my truck. I called her and said very politely, "Why the -beep- is my adapter gone from my truck?" She said, "Oh, I have it right here!" "The problem is," I replied, "I need it right now, actually 5 minutes ago would have been better." Remember, in the movie industry, you cannot serve your meal late or you are fired. So, my boss drove the adapter to me in a hurry - with 8 minutes to spare before dinnertime. I started cooking 80 T-bones "à la minute", knowing that the crew was on their way over... Once dinner was announced, 120 people ran full speed to our truck and ordered both the T-bone

<u>and</u> crab... After the meal, my assistant and I looked around - it was as if someone had taken the truck and flipped it upside down and placed it back on its wheels. And we felt like we had been in it! The best thing was that most of the members of the crew did not notice a difference. From that day, we referred to our job as "extreme catering".

The Canteen trucks are simple; they bring the food to workers that can't leave work, or to those who work in a remote area of town. You will have 100% freedom to cook whatever you want, as long as you keep cost controls on target. Also, one only little tiny problem: your customers are not exactly ready to eat a butter-poached salmon with asparagus risotto at work. So you will cook whatever you want... as long as you can sell it! If you cook inside a truck, it can also be challenging, but it should be fun.

Schedule is dictated by your itinerary for the day, similar to movie catering. A normal day may start at 4 or 5 am and finish around 1 or 2 pm. You need to cook lunch, and be ready to drive around to every place you serve during lunchtime... so just like movie catering, timing is extremely important in that business. I can recall a day working on a truck where I had to go across town to serve breakfast. I got to the central warehouse at 3:30am where 3 trucks would load up their supplies each morning. So, one morning I could not find my meat order, which was supposed to be arriving the night before. I started looking in every fridge for my meat and found nothing, so I went to check out the invoices to find out that it had been delivered the night before. At that point I started suspecting the other two Chefs who often would forget to make their own meat order and take whatever they could find. I looked in their trucks and found nothing. So, the only place it could be was inside the production kitchen, a place my boss kept under lock and key. I was reaching my limits of patience when suddenly I got an idea. I did not have the key, but I strongly believed that my meat had been put inside that kitchen by mistake. By then I was running late and could not waste any more time, so I took the door off the hinges with a screwdriver and hammer, placed the door nicely on the wall next to entrance and, sure enough, got my meat and went on with my day.

When I got back from my day around 6 pm, my boss was freaking out - telling us that someone had broken into the kitchen the night before. I looked at her and said, "It was not last night, and it was this morning." She said, "How do you know?" "I know because it was me that did it. My meat was inside your fridge, so I went in and got it!" I don't have to tell you, she was not impressed, but neither was I that morning. The good thing is, I got my own key after that...

Another unique thing to remember is that part of your day will be trouble shooting - stoves and restaurant equipment are not designed to be transported in a truck everyday. Expect 25% of your time to be spent fixing problems with your equipment, and have a good towing and repairman on your phone's speed dial.

The money is not so good to OK, but if you own the truck, it can be interesting money.

You can meet lots of people and get the rewards from your customers the very next day when you come back. If you cook from a central kitchen, and trucks come to you to get the food, your work becomes more like working in a cafeteria.

The hotel banquet and restaurant kitchens are a great way to get experience and try more than one thing at the same time. Often the great hotels have acquired reputations for their restaurants and/or banquets. You should at some point experience the preparation and service of a large hotel 1500 people banquet. It is a great chance to see the full orchestration of labour at is best. Hotels are often unionized and have many kitchen departments - like pastry, butcher, garde-manger and banquet. In high-end hotels, the banquet department has their own kitchen and crew, but the other departments' cooks are often asked to help out for big events. The schedule for banquets is dictated by the event, which could be sometimes brunch, lunch, or dinner.

One great thing about banquets it is that you often don't make the same menu two days in a row. The bad thing is it's hard to plan how much food to cook since you cannot use it tomorrow. The leftovers often go to the staff cafeteria, or the city community mission. The money is not so good to great, depending on the hotel. Big and small hotels sometimes have nice restaurants, and sometimes not!

The restaurants inside the hotels are sometimes independently owned, but in most cases hotels own and operate them. In the old days, the restaurants inside the hotel did not have to make profits, as the rooms made much of the money. Now, with times changing, the hotels have to be efficient from the penthouse to the basement. Hotels in general make lots of money with the rooms, so the restaurants inside rarely run out of capital money to do renovations. The downside is now restaurants also need to make their own profits, which puts pressure on the Chef! Many of the best restaurants in America have a hotel attached to them. These concepts often hire Chefs with a great reputation to bring in more guests for the hotel. It is a great place for you to find a mentor that would be willing to make you his (or her!) apprentice.

The resort life is not for everyone. If you choose to work in a resort, you should know a few things. These towns are made to accommodate tourists, not workers, so keep in mind that most necessities will cost you more than in the city. Whether you go to a winter or summer resort, you will find that often these resorts have a transient work force that comes and goes with the seasons. This scenario creates large staff turnover and many job openings. The work can be very challenging and it is often a great place to learn skills while enjoying your surrounding area. Cook at night, and hike or surf during the day!

There are resorts all over the world and they can offer great traveling experiences combined with the ex-patria money package. Take advantage of this opportunity while you are young and single.

Your schedule is going to be simple: work first, then fun after... In some places you will work so much that you may not have much time to enjoy the great outdoors. Resorts usually have hotels, and hotels have guests, and those guests have needs 24-7. You may work days, nights, graveyard, or you may even alternate between all of these shifts. Money can be great to amazing... once you make it to the top - "Executive Chef" - but until then you will be making OK to very good money. Resorts offer one big advantage for your career that mom and pop restaurants cannot offer, and that is they are usually big and they have many kitchen positions available. You should be able to rotate stations from time to time and learn even more.

I moved with my wife to Banff, Alberta, to work at the prestigious Banff Springs Hotel. This hotel is in the middle of a national park, surrounded by the beautiful Rocky Mountains, with a million dollar view for everyone to see for free.

Fishing with my wife was one of the perks of working in a national park! In 2002, I went fishing with my wife for the first time, and we had a blast! We drove 45 minutes towards Lake Louise to this great isolated spot in the mountains. We got there around 8:30am, and it looked like it was going to be hot. We hiked 1.6 km up a small mountain to find this amazing remote lake at the top. We both got dressed up in our waders, and started fly-fishing next to each other. After a few catches, the sun came out and the fish started to be a bit lethargic and not biting as much, but my very well-organized wife had planned for this scenario. She started sun bathing while I kept looking for dinner!

I really enjoyed my time at the resort. I cooked, I fished, and I advanced my career all at the same time.

I loved the work life in a resort, but I would have preferred to be a touch younger, instead of being ready to settle, which is harder to do in an area with higher prices and often less land.

The Spa is about health foods, special diets, allergies and detoxification. You will be asked to create light menus with dishes that are wheat-free, or sugar-free, and sometimes you may be asked to make green sauces with wheatgrass. Overall, you will need a fairly good knowledge of health food. The health conscious customers may seem very demanding to you, but really it's just up to you to make an adjustment into your work habits. The schedule is done with 3 meals a day, after tea/snack and some times special events. The money can be ok to great, depending on the reputation and size of the spa and how popular or busy it gets. Many spas have locations or affiliations in Europe and across the world, so there may be some opportunities to relocate somewhere very nice and make great money with the ex-patria money package.

The Banquet Halls and Convention Centers are for the lover in you! Working on lots of weddings can be fun, unless Chloae, you are single and looking to find a husband to give me grand children! But seriously, convention centers often offer a great chance to work on massive banquets. This type of concept doesn't operate like restaurants, however, as there is no daily business unless it's a banquet. Usually, the menu is individually made to fit the needs for each event, compared to restaurant concepts, which only have one menu for everyone.

In 2000, I worked in a convention centre. The menus were awesome and the organization was worth seeing at least once. Large weddings, conferences, corporate events or trade shows –I saw it all. It was nice work and a great experience. Anything from small to large banquets, and the food was ordered fresh just for those events. We would use up most of the food, and started fresh for the next banquets. Schedule was part-time on call for everyone, except with 4 permanent cooks plus the Chef. The money for the cooks was ok to good, but the Chef made great money. It was great for most cooks, since we all had full-time jobs aside from the convention work. So it gave us a few days of work with extra money to spend on toys.

The private clubs and golf clubs are both places where you can see great menus. Those two concepts will cater to similar crowds, and offer similar menu options. Many private events are catered at clubs like this, as they offer great food and often, great locations. The schedule can be seasonal for the golf clubs, but sometimes the club area is open year around. You could work breakfast, lunch, and dinner, weekends included. The money is OK to good, and in some cases, the Chef may make great money. It offers different possibilities; a great place to work part-time on call as a second job, or full time if you wish. AND, possibly improve your golf swing.

The Army Kitchens... Picture this: you're making a hollandaise sauce while being shot at with a Bazooka by the enemies. If this sounds good to you, go for it! Not unionized, but hierarchy rules. To be recruited, you will have to pass physical and mental tests, just to show that you are semi-normal. Then if you pass these tests, and depending on the country, you can start your 4-12 week training to become a soldier. Only after that can you start cooking. Even if you have already finished your cooking school, you will be trained the army way. Your everyday customers will have received countless hours of training in the art of killing someone in silence. You will feed them meals everyday and you better hope that they like their steak! Whether you cook at the army base, or in the field, you will cook meals for groups from fifty to thousands of people. The Tactical mobile kitchen vehicle is fully equipped to withstand shaking in rough terrain! You will be trained in fire fighting, nutrition, ration accounting and menu making. Stamina comes to mind! You must be flexible on your schedule requests in this job; I really don't think that you have any say in which days off you get! Money should be OK to good and when you leave to find a job in the civilian world, you will be regarded as a serious Chef. Once you are working, the good thing is, if your cooks don't respect you, you can kick their sorry butts!

Airline catering, although less popular, is still relatively busy; many airlines still serve meals on commercial planes, and private jets may have a Chef, too. Corporate airline kitchens have huge responsibilities to take care of multiple nationalities. Try to imagine the potential repercussions if a company would allow food poisoning to happen on a plane. The countries involved, the media coverage, and obviously, the scene with your boss: "you are so fired right now..." Any company that deals with international customers the way airlines or cruise ship companies do has to be extremely organized. The level of kitchen hygiene is very high, the temperature of raw or cooked food is monitored very carefully and the transport of each meal has to be done with extreme precision. Most of those kitchens are unionized, and have cooks that have been working there for a very long time. Your schedule is going to be changeable to begin with as the last one in, but it should stabilize after a few years. Money is OK to good, with some exceptions where you reach great money. The food is fresh and simple for the economy class, and more elaborate for the business and first class. There is not much creativity left here for the cooks. The Chef is most definitely a great administrator, with systems in place to be able to monitor the kitchen inch by inch and by the minute. Overall, this is a great place to learn and perfect your management techniques while still keeping your hands in the food.

The summer camps are great, if you would like to cook for 100 to 300 screaming kids. Just make sure that you have a deep fryer and everything will be fine! This can be a great summer job to match with a ski resort job in the winter.

The food is going to be simple, with still some room to be creative. The schedule in the kitchen is going to be busy everyday, but it's only a working boom for a few months, and then you're off. The money is not so good to OK, with some exceptions of course. I would think that working in a camp full of kids would keep you young at heart, maybe the perfect place to find out how much fun it would be to have kids of your own.

The oilrigs, and bush camps are just the thing if you are trying to stay away from civilization. Working in those camps creates huge responsibilities for the kitchen. Not only do you have to feed people, but also like many other job you are also responsible for the crew's mental health. Think about it - your meals are the highlight of their day. So, you had better make sure that you keep it interesting, or they can just throw you off the rig, or hide your body in the deep bush. Jokes aside, the Chef and cooks are of great importance to everyone in those camps, just as in any intense work environment. You have to be organized to work in camps. You cannot just run to the store and get a carton of cream if you need one. Ordering has to be done well and you have to make sure that your menus are well planned ahead of time. Schedules are simple; you work when you are at the camp. It varies from one industry to the other, but for oil drilling camps on land for example, you would work 6-8 weeks and be off 6-8 weeks. Money can be OK to great, and you won't have many places to spend it while you work. Here is a great place to learn to work hard and practice all your culinary skills.

The heli-ski Chef, talk about being a Chef at the right place! Cook two meals per day - breakfast and dinner - and ski in the most remote locations the rest of the day. If you ski or snowboard, this position is for you. You are usually picked up by helicopter and transported to your camp where you will cook for a dozen people or so. It is up to you to make menus, grocery lists, do all preparation, cook and clean the dishes.

Your schedule is early to late, and most of the time, you will do contract work alternating with someone else every couple weeks. Money is good, but remember, it's only in the winter... Many Chefs do heli-skiing in the winter and work for a golf course or summer camp in the summer! If you like flying, skiing, cooking and meeting new people, this is right for you. (Another job that tends to work best for the younger, single folks.)

The B&B (bed and breakfast) is simply like cooking for a few friends, except it's usually new friends everyday.

You need to plan menus, cook from your limited "home kitchen" (sometimes they can have professional equipment) and serve your guests at the table. Basically, your work is never done, you always have some prep to do, something to cook, or you may even have to go fix the leaky toilet!

Your schedule will start early and should finish late, but with the right set up, it can be lots of fun. Money can be OK to good, but the advantages can be great. In the right location, you may operate 10 months a year and then you could travel for the other two months.

The food is obviously breakfast, but some B&B's offer lunch and/or dinner also. I have been to a few B&B's that serve great food and are very busy. I like the idea that I could operate a small dinner table for the locals and guests two nights a week. Either way, it is not very often that B&B's are not operated by the owner, so you may need to have your own B&B if this is the path you choose.

The sport stadium has one big benefit beside all the hot dogs you can eat... can you guess what it is? Being inside the building while your favorite band or sports team are performing can be a lot of fun. Many times unionized, but not always. The schedule will flex in accordance with the events happening.

The money is not so good to good, and the menus are usually very simple. Let's face it, people don't go see a hockey game and eat Stuffed Duck Breast served with a Lavender and Pinot Noir Jus. They would do the occasional banquets, so I still think that it could be great to cook there for a while, until you get to see a few basketball games anyway.

The mall food court restaurants can teach you to either to go back to school and become a computer geek, or find a better concept to work in. Since I am not much of a mall shopper myself, I kind of like to eat a burger while my wife goes shopping. So, it's nice that they have cooks willing to do those jobs. Your schedule will be mall hours, with some exceptions if the restaurant has its own access from outside. Money is not so good to OK, but you will always have your Christmas shopping done before anyone else in the family!

The office building's snack bar could be the best place to meet a future investor to help you buy your dream restaurant. Those concepts can be challenging food wise, as many office people that have special diets will see you everyday and constantly ask for special items that fit with their own diets. You can find some great little snack bars that will make gourmet sandwiches a la carte. This is also a great place to learn to make tasty soups. The schedule is built around office hours, again with some exceptions if they stay open on the weekend. The money is usually not so good to possibly good, but it can be nice to be home with your family at night... and that is worth lots of money to certain people.

The community mission kitchen will be gratifying but also very challenging. You often receive cooked food donated from restaurants all over the city. Often, you have to re-transform leftovers into another meal for many people. You will also encounter customers with funky personalities on a daily basis, but don't worry - you see those everywhere anyway! The schedule revolves around 3 meals a day, and the money, well you don't do this job for money, obviously. The best part about this is that when you go to bed at night, you can feel proud of what kind of cook you are. Money is not everything.

The cooking schools are a great choice for anyone who has the patience to take on head-first the youth of today. You would need to like the school environment, have the right personality and have a great repertoire of technical skills. Overall, the schedule is great, often day shifts with some nights, but mostly day. Money can be good to great, and benefits are also usually really good. You would need to complete your Chef papers and/or pastry papers and gain some work experience out in the real world before considering this choice. After these previous steps, you could do a teaching certificate and you would be a perfect candidate for a culinary school teaching job. Some schools will require a "CCC" (Certified Chef de Cuisine) diploma.

PART FOUR
THE SANDWICH

Wrapping up

I suddenly wake up with a fast heartbeat... She does not want to be a Chef! I was dreaming! "What a relief," I muttered, "She can still become an astronaut and be the first female to walk on the moon." That morning I decided that I needed to write this book for her, just in case she did decide to become a Chef! And maybe it would help a few other people in the world too!

Dear Chloae,
I want to emphasize that 99% of the warnings and words of advice in this book are true, and the other 1% are not totally false! These situations and/or events really happen and they still happen everyday to a lot of cooks and Chefs. Like many before me, I had to learn about all this the slow and painful way over the years. Luckily for you, you don't have to do this - just read this book over and over until you have really captured the bulk of it. I am not trying to shelter you from learning by yourself,

but I have tried to let you know about some of the BS and also some of the good stuff that happens in the culinary world. Once in while, you will still make mistakes and forget about the warnings in this book, and that's OK! Knowing all this ahead of time will only allow you to improve your chances of becoming a great Chef and/or help you get better, smarter and faster than many hoodlums working in the kitchen with you.

Please remember, be good to yourself and respect others. All cooks, servers, bartender or dishwashers all have the same goal as you, it is to finish their work day, make some money and go home to see their loved ones.

Over the years, I have found myself cooking dinner for others while I was not able to cook for you. If I could change something, I would have liked to cook more for you and less for others.

In 2000, year of the millennium, Kristin and I got married. The wedding was simple, fun and I barely remember the food. The cake... wow, I do remember finishing the wedding cake with you at home. You and I decorated it with fresh flowers and we had to empty the entire fridge just to be able to fit it in... It was nice to be in the kitchen with you doing something I love, with someone I love.

My career choice to be a Chef took me all over, and without it, I may have never met my wonderful wife or have a beautiful and smart daughter like you. I can say today, I am a Chef and I am proud of it! If you choose to cook for a living, well so be it, I just hope that it brings you as much love, fun, excitement, adventure and great memories as it did for me. The way I see it, nothing will ever be good enough for my only daughter, but the truth is that I would probably love it if you followed this career path.

I really hope that this book helps you in making a sound decision; I have no regrets; I would just like my daughter to stop growing up and stay that little girl who has no worries or bills to pay!

Even if you don't take this career path, if you were to complete culinary school, you would be left with the greatest gift of all. You will have the power to feed yourself, friends and family really great meals, creating memories that will last you forever!

With love,
Papa

References of books that I strongly suggest you read:

Jacque Pepin "The Apprentice"

Stephen R. Covey "The 8th Habbit"

Michael E. Gerber "The E-Myth Manager"

Lance Armstrong "Biography"

Anthony Bourdain "Kitchen Confidential"

The only cookbook you'll ever need: Dornenburg & Page "Culinary Artistry"

Robert Heller "Negotiating Skills"

Bob Nelson, "1001 Ways to Energize Employees"

Bob Nelson, "1001 Ways to Reward Employees"

Joel Kurtzman, Glenn Rifkin, Victoria Griffith "MBA in a BOX"

ORDERING BOOKS from within the UK and EU countries:
Trafford Publishing (UK) Limited - Order Desk
9 Park End Street, 2nd floor
Oxford, UK   OX1 1HH
local rate number 0845 230 9601
phone 44 (0)1865 722 113   fax 44 (0)1865 722 868
email orders.uk@trafford.com

ORDERING BOOKS from any other country including the USA and Canada:
Trafford Publishing order desk
6E - 2333 Government Street,
Victoria, BC, Canada V8T 4P4
toll-free 1-888-232-4444
phone 250-383-6864   fax 250-383-6804
email orders@trafford.com

ISBN 1412070b8-b

Made in the USA